FREUDIANISM
A Marxist Critique

FREUDIANISM
A Marxist Critique

V. N. Vološinov

Translated by
I. R. TITUNIK
Department of Slavic Languages and Literatures
University of Michigan
Ann Arbor, Michigan

and edited in collaboration with
NEAL H. BRUSS
Department of English
University of Massachusetts—Boston
Boston, Massachusetts

ACADEMIC PRESS New York San Francisco London
A Subsidiary of Harcourt Brace Jovanovich, Publishers

ACADEMIC PRESS, INC.
111 Fifth Avenue, New York, New York 10003

United Kingdom Edition published by
ACADEMIC PRESS, INC. (LONDON) LTD.
24/28 Oval Road, London NW1

Library of Congress Cataloging in Publication Data

Voloshinov, V   N
      Freudianism.

      Translation of Frejdizm; kriticheskii ocherk.
      Includes bibliographical references and index.
      Appendices (p.   ):   I. Voloshinov, V.N.
Discourse in life and discourse in art.—II.
Bruss, N.H.   V. N. Voloshinov and the structure of
language in Freudianism.
      1.   Freud, Sigmund, 1856-1939.   2.   Subconscious-
ness.   3.   Sex (psychology)   4.   Communism.
I.   Title.
BF173.F85V6413   150'.19'52   76-14458
ISBN 0–12–723250–8

Contents

Preface

The Russian semiologist V. N. Vološinov's *Freudianism* would have been prophetic enough had it gone no further than to gloss the major texts of psychoanalysis with the principles of that structuralism which in the later 1920s Vološinov himself was forging. It would have been all the more prophetic had it merely engineered the most meager convergence of Marxism, psychoanalysis, modern linguistics, poetics, and stylistics, and more prophetic yet in anticipating specific major conclusions of the rediscovery of Freud by Vološinov's structuralist successors in France a generation later.[1] But, in fact, *Freudianism* is more than even a major icon in the history of ideas, for its insights are as independently rich and suggestive today both for psychoanalysis and for the theory of language as when it was written. Moreover, they are critical insights, their recognition demanding a change in the manner in which the fundamental principles of psychoanalysis, and linguistic theory as well, are understood.

Vološinov went to the root of Freud's theory and method, arguing that what is for him the central concept of psychoanalysis, "the unconscious," was a fiction. He argued that the phenomena that were taken by Freud as evidence for "the unconscious" constituted instead an aspect of "the conscious," albeit one that deviated ideologically from the rest of it, an "unofficial conscious" at odds with a person's "official conscious." For Vološinov, "the conscious" was a monologue, a use of language, "inner speech" as he called it. As such, the conscious participated in all of the properties of language, particularly, for Vološinov, its social essence. And thus Vološinov could argue that the unconscious was linguistic in nature because it was actually an aspect of the conscious, and, in turn, that it was a social phenomenon because it was linguistic. This type of argumentation stood behind Vološinov's charge that Freudianism presented humans in an inherently false, individualistic, asocial, and ahistorical setting.

It is a somewhat tenuous presentation, an admittedly "popular" study presenting oversimplified or caricatured versions of Freudian concepts, such as the depiction of the psychoanalytic therapy session as a confession with the therapist as inquisitor. Vološinov relied on a limited reading of Freudian texts,

---

[1] For a discussion of Vološinov's critique of Freud and the French structuralist reappraisal in the work of Jacques Lacan, see Appendix II of this volume, "V. N. Vološinov and the Structure of Language in Freudianism."

ignored Freud's own revaluations of central concepts, and, most important, failed to recognize the wealth of linguistic insight in Freud's works. In fact, a sensitivity to language, which Vološinov found lacking in Freud, came to be the very aspect of the Freudian texts on which contemporary French structuralists based their praise. Nonetheless, the strengths of Vološinov's approach and perspective overshadow the limitations of the work, and they derive from a concept of discourse that binds humans together in their social contexts of action and history through language.

For Vološinov, discourse is language in exchange between interlocutors, constituting the "scenario" of their actions. Coded into the speech of the discourse are social evaluations attached to the interaction between speaker, hearer, and content (which is termed "hero" in "Discourse in Life and Discourse in Art," appearing in translation as an appendix to this volume). A recognition of these values was a necessary condition for understanding an utterance, and it was the task of a Marxist sociology to explicate them. They were often manifest in so seemingly ephemeral a feature of speech as intonation, which necessitated that discourse be studied as a whole. As he stated in "Discourse in Life and Discourse in Art":

> The meaning and import of an utterance in life . . . do not coincide with the purely verbal composition of the utterance. Articulated words are impregnated with assumed and unarticulated qualities. What are called the "understanding" and "evaluation" of an utterance . . . always encompass the extraverbal pragmatic situation together with the verbal discourse proper. Life, therefore, does not affect an utterance from without; it penetrates and exerts an influence on an utterance from within, as that unity and that commonness of being surrounding the speakers and that unity and commonness of essential social value judgments issuing from that being without all of which no intelligible utterance is possible. Intonation lies on the border between life and the verbal aspect of the utterance; it, as it were, pumps energy from life situation into the verbal discourse, it endows everything linguistically stable with living historical momentum and uniqueness. Finally, the utterance reflects the social interaction of speaker, listener, and hero as the product and the fixation in verbal material of the act of living communication among them [p. 105–106].

The discourse model is at the heart of the most radical contention of *Freudianism:* that virtually the entire psychosexual apparatus of psychoanalysis could be replaced beneficially by a semiotics with a sociological interface.

The contention would perhaps seem more daring if contemporary French structuralists had not themselves discovered such a semiotics in Freud, but the discourse model itself was part of the legacy that made the discovery possible. The structuralist theory of discourse has had its own history. Vološinov, in extending the concept to thought and works of art and incorporating social value within it, took it beyond what was already present in Saussure's *Course.* Vološinov's contemporary, Roman Jakobson, fulfilled the promise of the concept in his model of six "constitutive functions in any speech event" (addresser, addressee, context, message, contact, and code), each corresponding to one of "six basic functions of verbal communication" (emotive, conative, referential, poetic, phatic, and metalingual), which participate with relative degrees of dominance in all utterances. What was a central feature of discourse for Vološinov, that it taps directly into the social values of a community, was pursued by such members of the Prague School of structuralism as Petr Bogatyrev and Jan Mukařovský. The embodiment of discourse features in grammar has been studied by Jan Firbas, and, in a less direct line of descent from Vološinov, by M. A. K. Halliday. Thus in the work of contemporary French structuralists, the concept of discourse is widely enough elaborated to be a given: for example, in Kristeva's criticism, as an object for "deconstruction" in Derrida's analysis of writing and texts, and especially in Barthes's analysis of codes in literature and culture and Lévi-Strauss's diachronic studies of signification in anthropological artifacts. Most telling for Vološinov's use of the discourse model to criticize Freud has been the aphorism under which the French structuralist rediscovery of Freud was motivated by the psychiatrist Jacques Lacan: "the unconscious is the discourse of the Other."[2]

A sign of the epistemological appeal of the idea of discourse is its appearance in the 1950s in the work of the French phenomenologist Maurice Merleau-Ponty. Phenomenology has been an intellectual orientation concurrent with and independent of structuralism, and yet, through the use of the concept of discourse, Merleau-Ponty's statements succeed in strongly evoking Vološinov's previously cited remarks on the "unity and commonness of being surrounding the speakers." Merleau-Ponty states:

> ... because, above all, language is not just the counterpart or replica of the affective context, it plays a role in it, introducing other motives, changing the internal

[2] Ferdinand de Saussure, *Course in General Linguistics,* trans. Wade Baskin (New York: McGraw-Hill, 1959), pp. 11–17; Roman Jakobson, "Concluding Statement: Linguistics and Poetics," in *Style in Language,* ed. Thomas A. Sebeok (Cambridge, Mass.: MIT Press, 1969), pp. 350–377. For sources on the Prague School, see Ladislav Matejka and I. R. Titunik, eds., *Semiotics of Art* (Cambridge, Mass.: MIT Press, forthcoming); Jan Firbas, "On the Concept of Communicative Dynamism in the Theory of Functional Sentence Perspective," *Sbornik Prací Filosofické Fakulty Brněnské University, A: Řada Jazykovědna* 19(1971): 135–144; M. A. K. Halliday, *Explorations in the Functions of Language* (London: Edward Arnold, 1973); Julia Kristeva, "The System and the Speaking Subject," in *The Tell-Tale Sign,* ed. Thomas A. Sebeok (Lisse, Netherlands: Peter de Ridder, 1975), pp. 47–55; Jacques Derrida, *L'Écriture et la différence* (Paris: Seuil, 1967); Roland Barthes, *S/Z,* trans. Richard Miller (New York: Hill and Wang, 1974); Claude Lévi-Strauss, *Structural Anthropology,* trans. C. Jacobson and B. G. Schoepf (Garden City, N. Y.: Anchor, 1963). For Jacques Lacan, see especially "Of Structure as an Inmixing of an Otherness Prerequisite to Any Subject Whatever," in *The Languages of Criticism and the Sciences of Man,* ed. Richard Macksay and Eugenio Donato (Baltimore: Johns Hopkins Press, 1970), p. 188.

meaning, and ultimately is itself a form of existence or a diversion within existence. . . . The relations with others, intelligence, and language cannot be set out in a linear and causal series: They belong to those cross-currents where *someone lives* (Merleau-Ponty's italics).[3]

Freudianism is itself an epistemological document. In the form of a critical reading of the history of Freudian theory through the concept of the unconscious, it maps out the domain of mind as the legitimate object of study of a nonreductive, discourse-based semiotics with a profound connection to Marxist sciences of society and ideology. Vološinov's condemnation of Freudianism as a decadent and popular cult ideology notwithstanding, Freudian psychology constitutes then and now an unequaled target for semiotic investigation of mind because it is expansive and comprehensive, self-contained and self-sustaining, and above all, as Vološinov noted, because it explicitly takes significations—language—as its data, perhaps as all psychologies ultimately must.

The epistemological statement that Vološinov made was, of course, that thought was a use of language. It is not a unique position; it is discoverable in such diverse forms as Noam Chomsky's discussion of grammars and innate ideas and Leonard Bloomfield's endorsement of logical positivism and behavioral psychology (also, perhaps to Vološinov's chagrin, in the work of a Romantic poet such as Shelley and an analytic philosopher such as Wittgenstein).[4] What is unique is the sophistication the statement attains in the critique of psychoanalysis, even within its limitations, and the alternative it yields. These results derive from the discourse model, which serve as Vološinov's theory of language. Despite its prevalence in structural thought, the discourse model still is deeply suggestive for linguistic theory.

Standard theories of language typically have treated other aspects of language only at the cost of avoiding or misrepresenting the actual world of language's use, the social context with which Vološinov was so concerned. Referential theories depict language as the aggregate of individual words, and take as its most important property that these words stand for nonlinguistic objects. Purely formal theories seek to define language as the regular (or irregular) alternation of minimal units of sound or information from which are formed words, sentences, and such higher-order structures as texts and internalized grammars. The two

---

[3] "The Problem of Speech," in *Themes from the Lectures at the Collège de France: 1952–1960,* trans. John O'Neill (Evanston, Ill.: Northwestern University Press, 1970), p. 21.

[4] Noam Chomsky, *Language and Mind* (New York: Harcourt Brace Jovanovich, extended edition, 1972); Leonard Bloomfield, *Language* (London: George Allen and Unwin, 1962), pp. 23–36, and essays in *A Leonard Bloomfield Anthology,* ed. Charles F. Hockett (Bloomington, Indiana: Indiana University Press, 1970); Percy Bysshe Shelley, "A Defence of Poetry," in *Selected Poetry and Prose,* ed. Carlos Baker (New York: Modern Library, 1952), pp. 494–522; Ludwig Wittgenstein, *Philosophical Investigations,* 2nd ed., trans. G. E. M. Anscombe (Oxford: Blackwell, 1967).

types of theories reduce out roles and relations among language users, circumstances of use, indices of intention, and other aspects of social context.

It took Peter Strawson's "On Referring" to show the limitations of referential theories.[5] After a history of futile attempts to find ways in which statements with no possible referents such as "The present King of France is bald" could be meaningful under referential theory, Strawson argued that meaningfulness was a function of the use of a statement, not solely of reference, and that it was not a property of sentences taken in abstraction. Strawson's basic insight, that humans use language for purposes other than to refer to things, seems extremely obvious in the light of Vološinov's stress on its ideological function, but a belief that the essence of language is reference was and is extremely deep-seated.

Similarly, it took generative semantics to show that even grammars of sentences must prominently employ the intentions and roles of language users in their explanations.[6] After unsuccessful attempts at grammar-writing based on formal relations of atomic elements of lexicon, word order, and inflection, generative semantics indicated that language could be explained formally only if features of use were counted among the aspects of form. The discovery, however, would not be unexpected in the light of Vološinov's work, which recognizes from the start the self-interested quality of language that the generative semanticists came to include in grammar.

The sociolinguistics of William Labov has revealed that the structure of language varies across class lines as distinctly as it varies across history.[7] Labov's work indicates that a given utterance could not be fully understood without a knowledge of not only the status of the speaker in his or her community but that of the hearer as well, for the utterance would be the product of a power relation between interlocutors. This would not be surprising, given Vološinov's emphasis on the sociological nature of language, its operation within the realities of class.

All this—a critique of Freud, an interdisciplinary semiotic investigation, an anticipation of structuralism, a discourse model, a theory of language—occurs within *Freudianism*. It is a richness independent of the scope of the work and the validity of specific arguments. It is not satisfactory, for example, for Vološinov to place against Freud's detailed exploration of psychical illness his own terse explanation of the psychopathologies as manifestations of conflict between "official" and "unofficial" consciousness at a historical moment when a long-ascendant social class goes into decline. (Works of verbal art, which Vološi-

---

[5] *Mind*, 59 (1950): 320–344.

[6] See especially John Robert Ross, "On Declarative Sentences," in *Readings in English Transformational Grammar*, ed. Roderick A. Jacobs and Peter S. Rosenbaum (Waltham, Mass.: Ginn, 1970), pp. 222–272.

[7] See especially *Sociolinguistic Patterns* (Philadelphia: University of Pennsylvania Press, 1972).

nov calls "a powerful condenser of unarticulated social evaluations," are explained in "Discourse in Life and Discourse in Art" as the product of a concord between the two aspects of consciousness.) Except for the historical input, Vološinov's diagnosis is at best only a meager terminological variant of Freud's own position. Yet the terminology of "official" and "unofficial" consciousness, supported as it is by "inner speech" and its ideological function and continuity, only enhances Freud's own work. *Freudianism* thus goes far beyond its own scope, even to the benefit of that which it condemns.

Extremely little information about V. N. Vološinov has come to light. As hard facts we know only that he was born June 18, 1895, in St. Petersburg (Leningrad), and that in 1934 he was residing in that same city and was a docent at the Herzen State Pedagogical Institute, a senior researcher at the State Institute for Speech Culture, and a member of the "scientific workers" section of the Soviet Academy of Science.[8] It is hardly to be doubted, although no documents on this matter are available, that he was also a member of the group of scholars and artists that gathered around M. M. Baxtin in Leningrad in the 1920s. The fate of M. M. Baxtin himself and of at least one other member of the circle, P. N. Medvedev, is known: Both were arrested sometime in the 1930s and both were "rehabilitated" in the 1960s (Medvedev posthumously).[9] About Vološinov's fate absolutely nothing is known or, rather, has been made public. At some point after 1934 he utterly vanishes. During the "thaw" period of the 1960s his name and references to his writings began to reappear in the Soviet press. However, the only information about the man himself was the identification of V. N. Vološinov as a member of the Baxtin circle ("student, follower and collaborator" of Baxtin) in a report of the meeting held at Moscow University in honor of M. M. Baxtin's 75th birthday.[10] Then, in 1973, the enigma of

---

[8] This information appears in *Nauka i naučnye rabotniki Leningrada*, Leningrad, 1934. From newly obtained information (see footnote 12) we also now know that Vološinov was a teacher at the Vitebsk Conservatory (Byelo-Russia) in the very early 1920s.

[9] Soviet encyclopedias now include both Baxtin and Medvedev but *not* Vološinov.

Our newly obtained source of information (see footnote 12) amplifies and corrects our oversimplified version of Baxtin's fate. We are told there that in 1929, after the publication of his book on Dostoevskij, Baxtin "settled [*poselilsja* !] on the border between Siberia and Kazakhstan in the town of Kustanaj. He spent about six years there, employed in local institutions [*služa v mestnyx učreždenijax* !]." In 1936 he moved to Saransk to take a post at the Mordovian Pedagogical Institute, leaving Saransk for Moscow sometime the following year. He returned to Saransk in 1945 and resumed his duties at the Mordovian Pedagogical Institute (later University of Mordovia) until reasons of failing health forced him to retire in 1961. This same source of information suggests that at no time, including his six years in Kustanaj, did Baxtin cease his scholarly activities.

[10] *Voprosy jazykoznanija* 2 (1971): 160–162.

Vološinov was given an extraordinary twist by the published declaration of the eminent Soviet philologist V. V. Ivanov that all the key writings of V. N. Vološinov (as well as a book by P. N. Medvedev) are actually the work of Baxtin himself, with Vološinov and Medvedev merely having served as editors and proofreaders—but with their names appearing on the title pages.[11] For this claim Ivanov supplies no proof, simply stating that there is "eyewitness testimony" to that effect and that the writings themselves (that is, the writings of Vološinov, Medvedev, and Baxtin, taken together) testify to the authorship of one man—Baxtin. Obviously, Ivanov must know more than he is willing or able to divulge at the present time, but as things now stand there is absolutely no reason to accept his claim at its face value. That claim introduces too many puzzles and oddities. For one thing, if Ivanov is correct, then Baxtin accomplished the extraordinary feat of authoring at least four books within the period 1926–1929, each book with a distinctly different field of investigation and set of research sources. In addition to books, Baxtin would also have written, during approximately the same period of time, at least three articles, of which one is in three substantial parts. To be sure, extraordinary productivity of this kind is neither impossible nor unknown in the scholarly world, but in this case a suggestion of dubiousness is unavoidable due to the accompaniment of other puzzles and oddities. For instance, *Marxism and the Philosophy of Language* (Vološinov; 1st edition 1929) and *Problems in Dostoevsky's Creative Art* (Baxtin; 1st edition 1929) both focus on the problem of reported speech or what is called in Russian literally "the speech of another" (*čužaja reč'*). While the same orientation toward this problem clearly underlies both books, the particular target of investigation in the former—"quasi-direct discourse" (*nesobstvenno prjamaja reč'*) is not mentioned at all as such in the central, theoretical chapter of the second work. Indeed, the terminological systems of the two books do not coincide in general. Furthermore, though this is hardly the place to attempt to prove it, the style of the articles and books signed by V. N. Vološinov strikes many readers as quite different from that of *Problems in Dostoevsky's Creative Art* (the only work signed by M. M. Baxtin published at the time). One must add to this list of evidence, of course, the obvious fact that the Marxist orientation (however unorthodox from certain points of view) that permeates all the writings signed by V. N. Vološinov (and Medvedev as well) is conspicuously absent from Baxtin's book. Finally, what is one to make of the fact that Ivanov's

---

[11] V. V. Ivanov, "Značenie idej M. M. Baxtina o znake, vyskazyvanii i dialoge dlja sovremennoj semiotiki" [The Importance of Baxtin's Ideas on Sign, Utterance, and Dialogue for Modern Semiotics], *Trudy po znakovym sistemam*, 6, Tartu (1973). The English reader will find a summary and discussion of this article in Dmitri Segal, *Aspects of Structuralism in Soviet Philology*, Department of Poetics and Comparative Literature, Tel-Aviv University, 1974, pp. 120–132.

list of works signed by Vološinov but supposedly written by Baxtin does not include the first, short version of *Freudianism*, a work that was incorporated almost wholly and verbatim into the later book and which, for reasons to be discussed in the Translator's Introduction, seems most unlikely to have been written by Baxtin?

Other puzzles and oddities could be cited, but this seems sufficient for present purposes. In short, it is not by any means impossible that what Ivanov claims is true—that Baxtin was "responsible" for writings signed by Vološinov and Medvedev, but until the difficulties that that claim generates are resolved the editors of the present volume must maintain, in all fairness and to the best of their knowledge and judgment, that the writings presented here in English translation are the works of Valentin Nikolaevič Vološinov.[12]

NEAL H. BRUSS
I. R. TITUNIK

[12] After this Preface had already been written and submitted for publication, an additional source of information came into our hands—a collection of essays in honor of M. M. Baxtin's 75th birthday and the 50th anniversary of his career as scholar and teacher: *Problemy poètiki i istorii literatury (Sbornik statej)* [Problems in Poetics and History of Literature (A Collection of Essays)], Saransk, 1973. The book contains a sketch of the life and work of Baxtin under the title, "Mixail Mixajlovič Baxtin, Kratkij očerk žizni i dejatel'nosti," written by V. Kožinov and S. Konkin, pp. 5–15. Regarding the working relationship of V. N. Vološinov (and P. N. Medvedev) with Baxtin we are told the following: "On the basis of conversations [Na osnove besed] with Mixail Mixajlovič devoted to problems in philosophy and psychology, philology and aesthetics, a number of articles and books were later composed" (p. 6). The footnote to this statement lists the books *Frejdizm* and *Marksizm i filosofija jazyka* by V. N. Vološinov and *Formal'nyj metod v literaturovedenii* by P. N. Medvedev and mentions "articles by V. N. Vološinov in journals and essay collections, as well." The bibliography of works by and about M. M. Baxtin appended to this sketch (pp. 16–19) does *not* include any works signed by Vološinov or Medvedev. The sketch was prepared by intimate acquaintances of Baxtin and published while the scholar was still alive. Some further details from this sketch are given in footnote 7 to the Translator's Introduction.

Acknowledgments

Albert Einstein, "On the Method of Theoretical Physics" is quoted on p. 122 from *Ideas and Opinions* by Albert Einstein, copyright 1954 by Crown Publishers, Inc. and used by permission of Crown Publishers, Inc.

The Standard Edition of the Complete Psychological Works of Sigmund Freud, revised and edited by James Strachey, are used in quotations with the permission of Sigmund Freud Copyrights, Ltd., the Institute of Psycho-Analysis, London, and The Hogarth Press Ltd. Quotations appear on pp. 124, 127, 132, and 141 from *The Interpretation of Dreams* by Sigmund Freud, translated from the German and edited by James Strachey, published in the United States by Basic Books, Inc., by arrangement with George Allen & Unwin Ltd. and The Hogarth Press Ltd. Permission to reprint from *The Interpretation of Dreams* has been given by George Allen & Unwin Ltd. Quotations (pp. 125-26, 131-33, and 138) are taken from essays appearing in *Collected Papers of Sigmund Freud* (Volume 4 and Volume 2 authorized translation under the supervision of Joan Riviere; Volume 3 authorized translation by Alix and James Strachey), published by Basic Books, Inc. by arrangement with The Hogarth Press Ltd. and the Institute of Psycho-Analysis, London. *Introductory Lectures on Psycho-Analysis* is quoted on pp. 52–54 and 56 with the permission of George Allen & Unwin Ltd; the material is also reprinted from *A General Introduction to Psycho-Analysis* by Sigmund Freud, authorized English translation by Joan Riviere, with the permission of the Liveright Publishing Corporation. Copyright 1920 by Edward L. Bernays. Copyright renewed 1948 by Joan Hoch, care of Liveright. Copyright © 1963 by Joan Riviere. *Jokes and their Relation to the Unconscious* is quoted on p. 132 with the permission of W. W. Norton and Co., Inc. and Routledge & Kegan Paul Ltd. *New Introductory Lectures on Psycho-Analysis* is quoted on p. 137 with the permission of W. W. Norton and Co., Inc.

Jacques Lacan, "The Insistence of the Letter in the Unconscious," translated by Jan Miel, is quoted on p. 140 with the permission of the editors of *Yale French Studies*. "The Function of Language in Psychoanalysis," translated by Anthony Wilden, is quoted on pp. 123, 130–31, 145, and 148 from Anthony Wilden, *The Language of the Self* (Baltimore, Johns Hopkins, 1968; New York, Delta, 1975). It is used with the permission of Anthony Wilden.

Herbert Marcuse, *Eros and Civilization*, is quoted on p. 142 with the permission of Beacon Press.

Maurice Merleau-Ponty, "The Problem of Speech" is quoted on pp. ix–x from *Themes from the Lectures at the Collège de France: 1952-1960*, translated by John O'Neill, and reprinted with the permission of John O'Neill and Northwestern University Press.

Guide to Transliteration

Russian names and words in the translated text and footnotes and in the appendices are transliterated in accordance with the standard scholarly system in which the following special signs have the approximate values indicated below:

' *soft sign,* indicating that the preceding consonant is "softened" (i.e., palatalized)

" *hard sign,* indicating that the preceding consonant is not palatalized

c *ts*

č *ch*

e *e,* as in *egg*

e *e,* as in *egg,* preceded by "j" as explained below

j *y* initially (before a vowel), terminally (after a vowel), medially between vowels or between hard or soft sign and a vowel; elsewhere indicates that the preceding consonant is palatalized

š *sh*

šč *shch*

x *h*

y *i,* as in *bill*

ž *zh*

Compare the following examples of certain Russian names in their common English spellings and their transliterated equivalents: Chekhov = Čexov, Dostoyevsky = Dostoevskij, Gogol = Gogol', Pushkin = Puškin, Tolstoy = Tolstoj, etc.

FREUDIANISM
A Marxist Critique

Translator's Introduction

In Russia, as everywhere throughout Europe and America during the early years of the twentieth century, Freud's psychoanalytical doctrine generated intense interest. The Freudian texts were translated into Russian, Russian commentaries burgeoned and proliferated, and Russian disciples set up practice.[1] Naturally, and again as everywhere else, this ferment of interest included the polemics of pro and con forces.

By no means did this activity cease or slacken with the advent of the Soviet regime, but the situation, especially in the latter half of the 1920s, acquired a new and urgent note: A number of eminent Soviet scientists not only expressed approval for at least the "scientific core" of psychoanalysis but even advanced the notion that it—that "scientific core"—"best corresponded to those requirements which Marxism makes incumbent upon a science of psychology [p. 17 of this book]." Such a claim aroused considerable and heated controversy, and energetic counterarguments on the part of fellow Marxists were not long in coming. Among the Marxist counterarguments that set out to prove Freudianism "totally unacceptable from an objective-materialistic point of view" was the book *Freudianism* by V. N. Vološinov, published in 1927.

Actually, *Freudianism* was the second such attempt by Vološinov: Earlier, in 1925, an article on Freud signed by the same author appeared in the journal *Zvezda* under the title "Beyond the Social."[2] Most of the text of this article was in fact incorporated into the later book, but a crucial difference between the article and the book consists in what the former did *not* contain. "Beyond the Social" is completely devoid of any theory of verbal discourse, any orientation at all toward the problem of language.[3] In 1925 the objective-materialistic

---

[1] An account (very biased but informative nevertheless) of the Russian and Soviet-Russian interest in Freud is given in the current standard work on history of Soviet psychology, A. V. Petrovskij, *Isotorija sovetskoj psixologii*, Moscow, 1967, pp. 79-94.

[2] "Po tu storonu social'nogo," *Zvezda* 5 (1925): 186-214.

[3] What is more, Freud's definition of the unconscious as the "nonverbal" was interpreted by Vološinov *at that time* as merely Freud's effort to compensate somewhat for his otherwise "metaphysical" concept of the unconscious. See *ibid.*, p. 203.

psychology that Vološinov upheld and opposed to Freud's "subjectivism" was exemplified fully by Pavlov's reflexology, J. Loeb's theory of tropisms, and other similar psycho-physiological trends. In that section of his polemic where he was obliged to point out the positive alternative to the unacceptable psychology of Freud, Vološinov writes:

> By the unconscious we can legitimately understand only some *effect-producing activity*, an energy or force (possibly psychical but equally possibly somatic in nature) that, once having emerged into consciousness—and only in and for the consciousness—acquires those forms and that content (perhaps obscure for the self-observing subject and more distinct for the interpreting analyst) which Freudianism without a qualm then *projects* into its so-called "unconscious" . . . .
>
> We believe that only a supposition of the sort we are postulating constitutes that essential minimum of hypothesis which adequately explains all the real empirical facts of human behavior that Freud and his disciples have come up with. And, of course, a science can admit only a minimum of hypothesis.
>
> How are we to conceive of this "effect-producing activity" that corresponds to the Freudian unconscious?
>
> Isn't there a risk of our falling out of the frying pan into the fire and coming up ourselves with an even more horrendous metaphysical substance to replace Freud's "id"?
>
> The reader can rest easy on this point. We have no inclination even to suppose some psychical energy in undifferentiated form; we believe that what is involved here are mechanisms of the same sort as have become familiar to us under the name of *reflexes* (Pavlov and his school), in part also *tropisms* (J. Loeb) and other chemisms—in short, processes of a purely somatic and material kind. In any case, it is only on this plane that scientific definitions of Freud's unconscious phenomena might be located. We are of course as yet unable to translate them into the language of scientific materialism but we do now know, at any rate, the direction in which such a translation could be made possible.[4]

How astoundingly different from this statement is the passage on this same matter in *Freudianism* where Vološinov, having duly acknowledged and praised the merits of the physiological approach, declares; "But when it comes to an explanation of human behavior all this [reflexology, tropisms, and so on] supplies us very little [p. 83 of this book]."[5]

Without knowledge of the facts—facts not likely ever to come fully to light—one can only speculate on the reasons for this remarkable change of view. Perhaps the Baxtin circle had not formed or perhaps V. N. Vološinov had not become one of its participants until after the publication of "Beyond the

---

[4] *Ibid.*, p. 202.

[5] It should be noted again that the article, "Po tu storonu social'nogo," is not listed by V. V. Ivanov as a work of Baxtin's. Yet, almost the entire text of this article was incorporated into *Freudianism*—a book that Ivanov of course does attribute to Baxtin. It is inconceivable that Ivanov was unaware of the earlier article.

Social." In any case, one is very tempted indeed to ascribe this change to the influence of the kind of thinking cultivated by the Baxtin circle[6-7]—an influence that must have had its effect very soon thereafter. The very next year, 1926, the article "Discourse in Life and Discourse in Art" appeared on the pages of the same journal, *Zvezda*, and unmistakably identified the author's cardinal orientation toward language, toward verbal discourse, or, literally translated from the Russian, "the word," as the key to the study of all ideological formations. Moreover, the basic concepts that were to transform the polemical "Beyond the Social" into the systematic treatise *Freudianism* were here distinctly registered: the intrinsically and inalienably *social* nature of language; the implementation of the communication model of addresser-message-addressee (in Vološinov's terms, speaker-hero-listener); the identification of inner and outward speech as different forms of one and the same phenomenon; the postulation of the utterance, or speech act, permeated through and through with "social evaluation," as the real unit of human speech; the notion of the unity of all ideological activity—the single chain from the most inchoate apprehension on the lowest levels of "behavioral ideology" to fully fledged, complex, and elaborate formations in law, art, religion, government—and so on. The connection with the leading ideas of the Baxtin circle, as evidenced (and curiously enough, only later) by P. N. Medvedev's *The Formal Method in Literary Scholarship: A Critical Introduction to Sociological Poetics* (1928) and Baxtin's *Problems in Dostoevskij's Creative Art* (1929), are patent and substantial.

In his masterwork of 1929, *Marxism and the Philosophy of Language*, V. N. Vološinov refers to his earlier study of Freud—the book *Freudianism*—as a "popular" essay, a work presumably meant for the public at large and not

---

[6]On the linguistic orientation of the Baxtin school, and of Vološinov in particular in the intellectual environment of the early twentieth century and its relationship with current trends, see L. Matejka, "On the First Russian Prolegomena to Semiotics," in V. N. Vološinov, *Marxism and the Philosophy of Language*, trans. L. Matejka and I. R. Titunik (New York and London: Seminar Press, 1973), pp. 161-174.

[7]In our newly obtained source of information (see Preface, footnote 12), V. Kožinov informs us of a Baxtin circle that existed in the very early twenties in the city of Vitebsk, Byelo-Russia, where Baxtin was living and working at the time. It is there, we are told, that Medvedev and Vološinov first met him and became his close friends and disciples (*učenniki*). We are also told that Baxtin returned to Leningrad in 1924. When Medvedev and Vološinov appeared in Leningrad is not clear. In any case, the Baxtin circle presumably reformed in Leningrad sometime after his return. Therefore, our conjecture, while incorrect regarding the chronology of Vološinov's acquaintance with Baxtin, is still possibly valid in the sense that the changes in Vološinov's thinking may have come about as the result of new concerns in the re-formed circle. At all events, "Beyond the Social" would certainly seem a work of the interim between the two circles.

merely for an audience of sophisticates or specialists. This characterization is somewhat misleading, however. That Vološinov operated with a much more complex, perhaps even devious, sense of his "listener," his addressee, is borne out, for instance, by the curious fact that the very same reader for whom the author feels obliged to gloss words such as *amnesia, uterus, penis, bisexual*, and the like is, at the same time, supposed to be able to take in, without the help of identification or explanatory notes, references to Kant, Nietzsche, Spengler, and even J.-C. Tetens. This peculiar "duplexity" of addressee has its effect on the style of the work, a style that is at once pedagogical and peripatetic, so to speak. Although all the glosses in the original have been omitted from the present English translation, the reader will no doubt be struck by this ambiguity in the relationship between the author and his audience—in itself a topic of special interest to Vološinov and one to which he devoted fundamental attention in *Marxism and the Philosophy of Language* and other writings.[8] This and other, doubtlessly related, features of Vološinov's style—his peculiar paragraphing, his repetitions of terms with different "tonality," his frequent recourse to conative and phatic signals (*of course, you see, to be sure*, and the like) have been preserved in the present translation.

The title of Vološinov's study of Freud in the original Russian is *Frejdizm: kritičeskij očerk*. It was issued by the State Publishing House, Moscow-Leningrad, 1927. Internal evidence makes it fairly certain that the work was actually completed in 1926. The first several chapters contain occasional footnotes by an editor (nowhere identified), obviously added in 1927. All such footnotes are labeled "Editor's note" in the present translation.

The original text consists of ten chapters, instead of the nine presented here. The final, tenth, chapter, devoted to a refutation of arguments by four Soviet scientists in favor of incorporating at least certain aspects of psychoanalysis into Marxism, has been omitted from the present translation on the grounds that it has little relevance to the interest that Vološinov's *Freudianism* retains for the present day. A number of Vološinov's footnotes referring to Russian translations of works by Freud and others have also been omitted.

The original title of the second work of Vološinov's included in this volume is "Slovo v žizni i slovo v poèzii: K voprosam sociologičeskoj poètiki." The text is found in *Zvezda*, No. 6, 1926, pp. 244-267.

The translator gratefully acknowledges his considerable debt to the co-editor of this volume, Neal H. Bruss, for reading the entire manuscript and making numerous helpful suggestions. Thanks are also due Bruce Kochis and especially Beth Forer for their generous help in doing library research.

---

[8]   *Marxism and the Philosophy of Language* , pp. 125-140, and, among other writings, Discourse in Life and Discourse in Art, pp. 93–116 of this book.

PART I

FREUDIANISM AND MODERN TRENDS
IN PHILOSOPHY AND PSYCHOLOGY
(CRITICAL ORIENTATION)

CHAPTER 1

The Basic Ideological Motif
of Freudianism

*Freudianism and the modern world. The ideological motif of
Freudianism. Similar motifs in modern philosophy. A preliminary evaluation of Freudianism.*

In 1893 a short article by two Viennese doctors, Freud and Breuer, appeared
on the pages of a professional journal of psychiatry.[1] The article, devoted to a
new method of treating hysteria through the use of hypnosis, was entitled by its
authors "On the Psychical Mechanism of Hysterical Phenomena (Preliminary
Communication)." From the kernel of this "preliminary communication" was to
develop one of the most popular ideological trends in modern Europe—psychoanalysis.

Inaugurated as a *modest psychiatric method*[2] with a barely developed
theoretical basis, psychoanalysis had, by the end of its first decade of existence,
already devised a *general theory of psychology* of its own that cast a new light
on all aspects of the mental life of man. Thereupon, work was undertaken to
apply this new psychological theory to the task of elucidating various domains
of cultural creativity—art, religion, and, finally, aspects of social and political
life. Thus, psychoanalysis succeeded in elaborating its own *philosophy of
culture*. These later postulations of psychoanalysis in general psychology and
philosophy gradually came to overshadow the original, purely psychiatric core of
the doctrine.[3]

---

[1] This article was later included in the book by J. Breuer and S. Freud, *Studien über
Hysterie* (1895; 4th ed., 1922).

[2] The method that Freud and Breuer proposed for treating hysteria was meant only to
supplement other methods already in medical use.

[3] Not all psychoanalysts would agree with this assertion, but it is true, nevertheless.
Freud's two recent books, *Jenseits des Lustprincips* (1920) and *Das Ich und Das Es* (1923),

Psychoanalysis achieved success among wide circles of the European intelligentsia even before World War I. After the war, and especially in recent years [the late 1920s], its influence reached extraordinary proportions in all the countries of Europe and in America. Owing to the breadth of this influence in the bourgeois world and among intellectual circles, psychoanalysis advanced to a position far beyond other contemporary ideological movements; Steiner's "anthroposophy" alone was possibly able to compete with it. Even such fashionable trends of the past as Bergsonism and Nietzscheanism had never, even at the height of their success, rallied so huge a body of supporters and "interested persons" as Freudianism.

The comparatively slow and, at first (up to 1910 approximately), very difficult progress of psychoanalysis en route to its "conquest of Europe" attests to the fact that this movement was no momentary and superficial "mode of the day," in the style of Spenglerism, but rather an abiding and profound expression of certain crucial aspects of European bourgeois reality. Therefore, *anyone wishing to fathom the spiritual physiognomy of modern Europe can hardly bypass psychoanalysis; it has become too signal and too indelible a feature of modern times.*[4]

How is the success of psychoanalysis to be explained? What is its attraction for a member of the European bourgeoisie?

Needless to say, it is not the specifically scientific, psychiatric aspect of the doctrine. It would be naive to suppose that masses of ardent devotees came to psychoanalysis through interest in the technical problems of psychiatry and through acquaintance with the professional publications in the field. That was not the way they encountered Freudianism. In the vast majority of cases, Freud was the first and last psychiatrist they read and *Internationale Zeitschrift für Psychoanalyse* the first and only professional journal of psychology whose pages they opened. It would be naive to suppose that Freud had somehow managed to engage the attention of vast circles of people to the technical issues of

---

are purely philsosophical in character. At the most recent International Congress of Psychoanalysts, in 1922, a great many participants expressed the apprehension that the speculative side of psychoanalysis had thoroughly overshadowed its original therapeutic purpose. On this point, see S. Ferenczi and O. Rank, *Entwicklungsziele der Psychoanalyse* (1924).

[4] One can judge how widespread the Freudian movement has become by the fact that there is now an entire international organization of Freudians. The Eighth Congress of Freudians was held in 1924 and was attended by representatives from various local groups in Vienna, Budapest, Berlin, Holland, Zurich, London, New York, Calcutta, and Moscow. There are now several periodical publications devoted to psychoanalysis and a special publishing house—the International Psychoanalytical Press in Budapest. The first psychoanalytical clinic for the indigent mentally ill was opened in Berlin in 1920. [*Editor's note* (See Translator's Introduction, p. 4. Translator)]

psychiatry. Obviously, neither was it practical interest in the achievements of a therapeutic method that made psychoanalysis attractive. It would be absurd to assume that all those masses of Freud's devotees were and are patients at psychiatric clinics eager for a cure. It is beyond doubt that Freud did succeed in striking a nerve in the modern bourgeoisie, but not through the specifically scientific or narrowly practical aspects of his doctrine.

Any ideological movement that is not the restricted property of some select group of specialists but encompasses wide and varied masses of readers who are obviously incapable of coping with the technical details and subtleties of the doctrine—any such ideological movement always allows of definition in terms of a *certain basic motif*, the *ideological dominant* of the whole system that determines its success and influence. This basic motif possesses a power of conviction and revelation all of its own and is relatively independent of the complex apparatus of its scientific foundation, to which the public at large does not have access. Therefore, this basic motif can be isolated and formulated in a rough and simple way without the risk of doing an injustice.

In this first—introductory—chapter we intend, somewhat anticipating our later exposition, to take up the task of singling out the basic ideological motif of Freudianism and providing preliminary evaluation of it.

We are guided in doing this by the following considerations.

Before the reader can be introduced into the rather complex and, at times, alluring labyrinth of the psychoanalytical doctrine, he needs to have a solid critical orientation given him. We must first of all show the reader in what philosophical context, that is, in line with which other philosophical currents that have held sway or still do hold sway over the minds of the European intelligentsia, he must perceive psychoanalysis so as to obtain an accurate notion of its ideological essence and value. That is the reason why it is necessary to feature the basic ideological motif of psychoanalysis. We shall see that this motif is by no means anything totally new or surprising, but rather that it is something that can be completely accommodated within the mainstream of all the ideological tendencies of bourgeois philosophy in the first quarter of the twentieth century—perhaps, indeed, the most striking and daring expression of those tendencies.

In the following chapter (Chapter 2), we shall endeavor to give the reader a similar critical orientation for viewing the purely psychological aspect of the Freudian doctrine, without as yet fully expositing that doctrine itself but acquainting the reader with the rivalry of various different trends in modern psychology. In this way we shall define the context within which the specifically psychological tenets of Freudianism should be viewed and judged.

Once the reader has been critically armed and made aware of the historical perspectives in which to view this new phenomenon, we shall proceed, starting with the third chapter, to a systematic exposition of psychoanalysis without recourse to critical commentary. In Part III of our study we shall return again to the critical themes noted in the first two chapters of Part I.

What, then, is the basic ideological motif of Freudianism?

A human being's fate, the whole content of his life and creative activity—of his art, if he is an artist, of his scientific theories, if he is a scientist, of his political programs and measures, if he is a politician, and so on—are wholly and exclusively determined by the vicissitudes of his sexual instinct. Everything else represents merely the overtones of the mighty and fundamental melody of sex.[5]

If a person's consciousness tells him otherwise about the motives and driving forces of his life and creativity, then that consciousness is lying. A *skeptical attitude toward consciousness* is an ever-present accompaniment to the development of Freud's basic theme.

Thus, what really counts in a human being is not at all what determines *his place and role in history*—the *class, nation, historical period* to which he belongs; only his *sex* and his *age* are essential, everything else being merely a superstructure. *A person's consciousness is shaped not by his historical existence but by his biological being,* the main facet of which is *sexuality.*

Such is the basic ideological motif of Freudianism.

In its general form this motif is nothing new and original. What is new and original is the elaboration of its component parts—the *concepts of sex and age.* In this respect Freud did genuinely succeed in disclosing an enormous wealth and variety of new factors and subtleties that had never before been submitted to scientific inquiry, owing to the monstrous hypocrisy of official science in all questions having to do with human sexual life. Freud so expanded and so enriched the concept of sexuality that the notions we ordinarily associate with that concept comprise merely a tiny sector of its vast territory. This must be kept in mind when making judgements about psychoanalysis: One ought not lose sight of this new and extremely expanded meaning of the term "sexual" in Freud, when, for instance, accusing psychoanalysis, as is commonly done, of "pansexualism."

Psychoanalysis has, furthermore, revealed much that is surprising also in the matter of the connection between sex and age. The history of a human being's sexual drive starts at the moment of his birth and proceeds to pass through a long series of individually marked stages of development that by no means correspond to the naive scheme of "innocent childhood-puberty-innocent old

[5] The author here emphasizes only the *basic* motif of Freudianism. From his later exposition (Chapter 3), the reader will learn that the doctrine on the existence of unconscious mental processes and on "resistance" and "repression" are equally integral parts of Freudianism (see Freud's article, "Psychoanalyse," in *Handwörterbuch der Sexualwissenschaft,* ed. M. Marcuse (Bonn, 1926), p. 614). [*Editor's note*]

age." The riddle about the ages of man that the Sphinx asked Oedipus found in Freud a unique and surprising solution. How sound a solution is another matter, one we shall take up later on. Here we need only note that *both component parts of the basic ideological motif of Freudianism—sex and age—are invested with thoroughly new and rich content.* That is why this motif, old in and of itself, has a new ring to it.

It is an old motif. It is constantly repeated during all those periods in the development of mankind when the social groups and classes that had been the makers of history are in process of being replaced. It is the *leitmotif of crisis and decline.*

Whenever such a social class finds itself in a state of disintegration and is compelled to retreat from the arena of history, its ideology begins insistently to harp on one theme, which it repeats in every possible variation: *Man is above all an animal.* And from the vantage point of this "revelation" it strives to put a new construction on all the values that make up history and the world. Meanwhile, the second part of Aristotle's famous formula—"man is a *social* animal"—is totally ignored.

The ideology of periods such as these shifts its center of gravity onto the isolated biological organism; the three basic events in the life of all animals—birth, copulation, and death—begin to compete with historical events in terms of ideological significance and, as it were, become a surrogate of history.

That which in man is nonsocial and nonhistorical is abstracted and advanced to the position of the ultimate measure and criterion for all that is social and historical. It is almost as if people of such periods desire to leave the atmosphere of history, which has become too cold and comfortless, and take refuge in the organic warmth of the animal side of life.

That is what happened during the period of the break-up of the Greek city states, during the decline of the Roman Empire, during the period of the disintegration of the feudal-aristocratic order before the French Revolution.

The motif of the *supreme power and wisdom of Nature* (above all, of man's nature—his biological drives) and of the *impotence of history with its much ado about nothing*—this motif equally resounds, despite differences of nuance and variety of emotional register, in such phenomena as epicureanism, stoicism, the literature of the Roman decadence (e.g. Petronius' *Satyricon*), the skeptical ratiocination of the French aristocrats in the seventeenth and early eighteenth centuries. *A fear of history, a shift in orientation toward the values of personal, private life, the primacy of the biological and the sexual in man*—such are the features common to all of these ideological phenomena.

And now once again, starting at the very end of the nineteenth century, motifs of the same kind have been distinctly voiced in European ideology. For twentieth century bourgeois philosophy the abstract biological organism has again become the central hero.

The philosophy of "Pure Reason" (Kant), of the "Creative I" (Fichte), of "Idea and the Absolute Spirit" (Hegel), that is, that which constituted the undeniably energetic and, in its way, respectable philosophy of the heroic age of the bourgeoisie (end of the eighteenth and first half of the nineteenth century), such philosophy still commanded a full measure of enthusiasm for history and organization (in the bourgeois style). In the second half of the nineteenth century this philosophy became increasingly diminished and gradually came to a standstill in the lifeless and static schemes of the "school philosophy" of epigones (neo-Kantians, neo-Fichteans, neo-Hegelians), finally to be replaced in our time by the passive and flabby "Philosophy of Life" with its biologistic and psychologistic coloration and its implementation of every possible shade of meaning and combination of the verb "to live."[6]

The biological terms for the various organic processes have literally deluged the modern Weltanschauung: Efforts are made to find biological metaphors for everything, so as to impart an agreeable animation to whatever the cold of Kantian Pure Reason had benumbed.

What are the basic features of this philosophy of the present day?

All thinkers of modern times, such as Bergson, Simmel, Gomperz, the pragmatists, Scheler, Driesch, Spengler, despite the many points and ways wherein they disagree with one another, are fundamentally united under the headings of three motifs:

1. *Life in the biological sense stands at the center of the philosophical system.* Isolated organic unity is declared to be the highest value and criterion of philosophy.

2. *Distrust of consciousness.* The attempt is made to minimize the role of consciousness in cultural creativity. Hence the criticism of the Kantian doctrine as a philosophy of consciousness.

3. *The attempt is made to replace all objective socioeconomic categories with subjective psychological or biological ones.* This explains a tendency to view history and culture as deriving directly from nature and to disregard economics.

Thus, Bergson, who still remains one of the most popular of European philosophers, posited at the center of his entire philosophical system the concept of a single *life force*—the *élan vital*, from which he endeavored to derive all forms of cultural activity. The higher forms of cognition (specifically, intuitive philosophical cognition) and artistic creativity were brought in line with *instinct*, which most fully expressed the unity of the continuum of life. The intellect, the creator of the positive sciences, was treated by Bergson with disdain, but

---

[6] See H. Rickert, *Die Philosophie des Lebens*. The book contains a good deal of information, but the author's point of view—that of an idealist-neo-Kantian—is unacceptable.

nevertheless he derived its forms also directly from the biological structure of the organism.[7]

The late Georg Simmel—a Kantian in his earliest works—became one of the twentieth century's most impressive exponents of fashionable biological tendencies. The *enclosed organic unity of individual life* came to stand for him as the highest criterion of all cultural values. Sense and meaning accrue only to those things that can be attached to that self-sufficient unity. In one of his fundamental works, *Individual Law*, Simmel endeavored to conceptualize ethical law as the law of the individual development of personhood. Taking issue with Kant, who required that ethical law have the form of *universality* (the categorical imperative), Simmel developed his own notion of an individual ethical law that is supposed to regulate not the relations of human beings in society but the relations of forces and drives within the enclosed and self-sufficient organism.[8]

The biologistic bent in philosophy has taken even cruder forms in the work of the pragmatists. Adherents of the late American psychologist William James, the father of the pragmatist movement, these people strive to reduce all types of cultural creativity to the biological processes of adaptation, expediency, and so on.[9]

A close resemblance of sorts to Freudianism is exhibited by the never-completed philosophical system of Freud's compatriot, the Viennese philosopher Heinrich Gomperz, called "Pathemperism." Gomperz attempted to reduce all categories of thought—causality, object, and so on—to feelings, to the emotional reactions of the human organism to the world. The influence of the Viennese sexologist, Otto Weininger, is detectable here.[10]

We find the same motifs, although in a considerably more complex form, in the thought of the most influential German philosopher of our day, Max Scheler, the chief representative of the phenomenological school. Scheler combines together the struggle against psychologism and primitive biologism and, thus, the advocation of objectivism, on the one hand, with deep distrust of consciousness and its forms and, thus, preference for intuitive modes of cognition, on the other. All positive, empirical sciences Scheler, in this respect

[7] Bergson's most important philosophical work is *L'Evolution Créatrice*.

[8] See Simmel, "Das individuelle Gesetz: Ein Versuch über das Prinzip der Ethik," *Logos* 4 (1913): 117-160. This work later appeared as a chapter in Simmels's last book, *Lebensanschauung* (1919). On Simmel, the Russian reader is referred to a brief article of Marxist orientation by Svjatlovskij appended to the translation of Simmel's *Conflicts of Modern Culture*—"Konflikty sovremennoj kul'tury," *Načatki znanij* (Petrograd, 1923).

[9] See James, *Pragmatism*, which is the basic philosphical work of the pragmatist movement.

[10] Gomperz's basic work is *Anschauungslehre*. Regarding Weininger's influence on him, see the Russian translation, *Učenie o mirovozzrenii* (Šipovnik Publishing House), pp. 172 175.

joining Bergson, derives from the forms of the biological organism's adaptation to the world.[11]

The ambition to subordinate philosophy to the needs and methods of the particular discipline of biology is most consistently expressed in the philosophical works of Hans Driesch, the well-known biologist-neovitalist, one of the founders of experimental morphology, who now occupies a chair of philosophy. The basic concept in his system is termed "entelechy," after Aristotle. Entelechy is supposedly the quintessence of organic unity and functionality. It governs all manifestations of the organism, its highest cultural activity as well as its lowest biological functions.[12]

Finally, let us make mention of the once-upon-a-time renowned but now almost forgotten attempt of Spengler to apply biological categories to the interpretation of the historical process.[13]

Thus, we see that the basic ideological motif of Freudianism is by no means its motif alone. The motif chimes in unison with all the basic motifs of contemporary bourgeois philosophy. *A sui generis fear of history, an ambition to locate a world beyond the social and the historical, a search for this world precisely in the depths of the organic—these are the features that pervade all systems of contemporary philosophy and constitute the symptom of the disintegration and decline of the bourgeois world.*

Freud's notion of the "sexual" is the extreme pole of this fashionable biologism. It gathers and concentrates in one compact and piquant image all the separate elements of modern-day antihistoricism.

What should be our attitude toward the basic theme of contemporary philosophy? Is there any substance to the attempt to derive all cultural creativity from the biological roots of the human organism?

[11] Among M. Scheler's works we shall name here only *Phenomenologie und Theorie der Sympathiegefühle* (Halle, 1913) and *Vom Ewigen im Menschen* (1920). There are no Russian works on Scheler with the exception of an article by Bammel', "Maks Šeler, katolicizm i rabočee diviženie" [Max Scheler, Catholicism and the Workers' Movement], *Pod znamenem Marksizma*, 7-8 (1926). A separate chapter is devoted to Scheler in our book, now being prepared for publication, *Filosofičeskaja mysl' sovremennogo Zapada* [Philosphical Thought in the West Today (there is no evidence that this book was ever actually published. *Translator*)]. A few pages of analysis and evaluation of Freudianism are included in the first of Scheler's works cited above.

[12] Driesch's basic work is: *Philosophie des Organischen*, 2 vols., (1909, one-volume ed., 1921). Others are: *Ordnungslehre* (1926), *Wirklichkeitslehre* (1924), and *Der Vitalismus als Geschichte und als Lehre* (1905). Among Russian Works on Driesch, see N. I. Kanaev, "Sovremennyj vitalizm" [Contemporary Vitalism], in *Čelovek i Priroda*, (Nos. 1-2, 1926).

[13] *Untergang des Abendlandes*, 2 vols. Marxist criticism of Spengler can be found in: Deborin, "Gibel' Evropy, ili toržestvo imperializma [The End of Europe or the Triumph of Imperialism], in *Filosofija i Marksizm (sbornik statej)* (GIZ, 1926).

The abstract biological person, biological individual—that which has become the alpha and omega of modern ideology—does not exist at all. It is an improper abstraction. Outside society and, consequently, outside objective socioeconomic conditions, there is no such thing as a human being. *Only as a part of a social whole, only in and through a social class, does the human person become historically real and culturally productive.* In order to enter into history it is not enough to be born physically. Animals are physically born but they do not enter into history. What is needed is, as it were, a second birth, a *social* birth. A human being is not born as an abstract biological organism but as a landowner or a peasant, as a bourgeois or a proletarian, and so on—that is the main thing. Furthermore, he is born a Russian or a Frenchman, and he is born in 1800 or 1900, and so on. *Only this social and historical localization makes him a real human being* and determines the content of his life and cultural creativity. All attempts to bypass this second, social, birth and to derive everything from the biological premises of the organism's existence are vain and doomed beforehand to fail: Not a single action taken by a whole person, not a single concrete ideological formation (a thought, an artistic image, even the content of dreams) can be explained and understood without reference to socioeconomic factors. What is more, even the technical problems of biology can never find thoroughgoing solution unless biology takes comprehensive account of the social position of the human organism it studies. After all, "the essence of man is not an abstraction inherent in each separate individual. In its reality it is the aggregate of social relationships."[14]

[14] From the *Sixth Thesis on Feuerbach*. [English translation quoted from *The German Ideology* (London: The Marxist-Leninist Library, 1942, vol. 17) p. 198. *Translator.*]

CHAPTER 2

Two Trends
in Modern Psychology

*Formulation of the issue. Experimental psychology. Objective
psychology. Verbal reaction. Marxism and psychology. The
psychological problem of Freudianism. Science and class.*

We are now acquainted with the basic motif of psychoanalysis and have
determined its intimate connection with other modern European ideological
trends. *This motif runs throughout the psychoanalysts' theories at all levels.* Of
course, it finds its clearest, ideologically most patent expression in a special
philosophy of culture, but even within the psychological doctrine, behind the
technical, specifically scientific apparatus of the system, we can discover *exactly
the same motif* functioning as the determinative principle of all of the Freudians'
notions about the mental life of human beings and the forces governing it.

Nevertheless, a fairly widespread opinion has it that, notwithstanding the
faultiness and untenability of its basic ideological motif, psychoanalysis still
does contain a sound, scientifically valuable core, which is, namely, its
psychological theory.[1] Proponents of this point of view maintain that the
technical psychological doctrine of Freud is completely compatible with a
different philosophical outlook and that, as a matter of fact, it best corresponds
to those requirements which Marxism makes incumbent upon a science of
psychology.

It is precisely in order to deal with this issue that we consider it essential,
before presenting an exposition of psychoanalysis, to provide the reader an
introduction on the topic of the basic trends in modern psychology and,
moreover, to make him aware of what the Marxist point of view might well
demand in regard to the methodological bases of this science.

---

[1] This is the point of view shared by Bykovskij, Zalkind, Fridman, Luria, and others.
[See note 9 below and Translator's Introduction, p. 4. *Translator*]

At the present time, both in Europe and here in the USSR, two trends in the study of the psychical life of humans and animals are engaged in spirited controversy. This is the _controversy between objective and subjective psychology_.

Each of these trends breaks down, in turn, into a series of individually marked tendencies. We shall identify only the most important of these in what follows, without going into the matter of their special and differential features. All that we really need is the basic distinction between the points of view of the subjectivists and the objectivists.

The variant of subjective psychology of most serious interest is Experimental Psychology (Wundt school, James school, and others—its major local representative is Professor Čelpanov), while the variants of objective psychology of similar weight are Reflexology (Pavlov school,[2] Bexterev[3] and others) and the so-called Science of Behavior, or Behaviorism, which is cultivated particularly in America (Watson,[4] Parmelee,[5] Dewey, and others). In the USSR, work in a direction similar to behaviorism is being done by Blonskij and Kornilov (Reactology).[6]

Now, what is the main source of disagreement between subjective and objective psychology?

Psychical life is accessible to human beings in two ways:

1. _Within his own self_ a human being directly, through _internal apprehension_, observes the occurrence of various mental experiences—thoughts, feelings, desires.

2. With regard to other people or to animals, he can observe only the _outward expression_ of psychical life in terms of the various _reactions_ of other organisms to stimuli. For _external apprehension_ there are, of course, no such things as desires, feelings, ambitions—after all, they cannot be seen or heard or touched; there are only specific material processes that occur in the reacting organism (i.e., in responding to stimuli). This outward material-corporeal

[2] I. P. Pavlov, _25-letnij opyt ob"ektivnogo izučenija vysšej nervnoj dejatel'nosti životnyx_ [Twenty-Five Years of Objective Study of the Higher Nervous Activity of Animals] (1926), _Lekcii o rabote bol'šix polušarij golovnogo mozga_ [Lectures on the Functioning of the Large Cerebral Hemispheres] (1927).

[3] V. M. Bexterev, _Obščie osnovy refleksologii čeloveka_ [General Principles of Human Reflexology] (Petrograd, 1923; 3rd ed., 1926).

[4] J. B. Watson, _Psychology from the Standpoint of a Behaviourist_ (London, 1919).

[5] M. Parmelee, _The Science of Human Behavior_ (New York, 1921).

[6] Kornilov, _Učenie o reakcijax čeloveka_ [Teachings on Human Reactions] (Moscow, 1921; 2nd ed., GIZ, 1927). Also his _Učebnik psixologii, izložennoj s točki zrenija dialektičeskogo materializma_ [A Textbook in Psychology from the Standpoint of Dialectical Materialism] (Moscow, 1926).

language of psychical life is, of course, observable by a human being with respect to himself, as well.

The question now is: Which of the two kinds of apprehension—internal-subjective or external-objective—ought to form the basis for a scientific psychology? Or might not some particular combination of the data of both serve that purpose?

We must first remark that no one any longer seriously defends pure subjective apprehension, without any admixture of data supplied by external apprehension, as the exclusive basis of psychology. What representatives of the contemporary version of subjective psychology now assert is that the basis of psychology can be provided only by *direct observation* of mental life (by *introspection*), but that its data must be amplified and controlled by external, objective observation. That is precisely the purpose an experiment serves, that is, an experiment is the deliberate causing of psychical phenomena, psychical experience, under predetermined external conditions erected by the experimenter himself.

This being the case, the makeup of such a psychological experiment in inevitably twofold:

1. One part of it, namely, the entire *external, physical situation* in which the experience under study occurs—the circumstances, the stimulus, the outward corporeal expression of stimulation, and the reaction of the subject—is located *in the field of the experimenter's external, objective apprehension*. This entire part of the experiment is amenable to methods of exact, natural-scientific ascertainment, analysis, and measurement with the help of special instruments.

2. The second part of the experiment—the psychical experience—is not present to the experimenter's external apprehension; indeed, it necessarily lies beyond any apprehension from outside. This part of the experiment is present only to the *internal apprehension* of the subject himself, who, in fact, reports the results of his *self-observation* to the experimenter. The subject's direct, *inner* data are then taken by the experimenter and placed in conjunction with the data of his, the experimenter's, own *external*, objective apprehension.

Clearly, the center of gravity of the whole experiment lies in its second, subjective part, that is, in the subject's inner experience; the experimenter's focus of attention is set precisely on it. This inner experience is, then, in point of fact, what psychology studies.

Thus, *in experimental psychology introspection has the final word*. Everything else, all those instruments for exact measurement, in which representatives of this trend take such pride, constitute only a mounting for introspection, an objective-scientific frame for a subjective-internal picture—and no more.

The question inevitably arises as to whether the "inner experience" of the subject does not in fact compromise the *integrity and consistency* of the experimenter's external apprehension. Does not this *inner point of view* (the subject after all reports his experience from an inner point of view) bring to bear *something incompatible with the data of external apprehension*, something fundamentally insusceptible to objective analysis and measurement?

That is precisely what the representatives of objective psychology maintain. They argue that it is impossible to construct an exact and objective science if the method of self-observation, which the subjectivists accept, is used. It is essential, they insist, that the point of view of external, objective apprehension be adhered to consistently and throughout if a scientific psychology is to be constructed. Meanwhile, the introduction of introspective data destroys the integrity and the consistency of external apprehension. Everything in life, everything in practice, that can have meaning must, after all, be presented as an external, material quantity, must be expressed in some purely material index of change.[7]

Such purely material quantities are the various *reactions of a living organism to stimuli*. Taken together, these reactions make up what we call the behavior of a human being or an animal.

This behavior of a living organism is wholly accessible to *external, objective apprehension*; everything of which it is comprised can be calculated, measured and brought into the necessary *cause-and-effect relation* with external stimuli and the conditions of the surrounding material environment. *Only this materially expressed behavior of the human and the animal can constitute the object of study in a psychology that wants to be exact and objective*. Such is the position of the objectivists.

A psychological experiment—for, of course, the objectivists, too, must use experiments—must be localized throughout its entire extent in the external world, and all its factors must be accessible to the experimenter. It is totally inadmissible for an objectivist to deal with the data of both internal and external observation *on one and the same plane* of material apprehension, as a subjectivist does. Inevitably *double formations* will arise, confusion set in, and the unity and integrity of external, material apprehension be undermined. The subject's "inner experience" must also be translated somehow into the language of external apprehension, and only in that shape can it be taken into account by the experimenter.

For *external* apprehension, what corresponds to inner experience are the subject's *words*, the words with the help of which he reports that experience.

---

[7] In the interests of accuracy, it should be noted that the behaviorists, while rejecting introspection as a scientific method of investigation, do, nevertheless, consider that, owing to the present state of psychology as a science, introspection should be used in certain cases where it is the only immediately available means of observation. See Watson, *Psychology*. [*Editor's note*]

This kind of expression of experience has been given the name *verbal reaction* (or "verbal account," in the terminology of the behaviorists).

Verbal reaction is a phenomenon of the highest complexity. It consists of the following components:

1. *The physical sound of articulated words;*
2. *Physiological processes in the nervous system and in the organs of speech and perception;*
3. *A special set of features and processes that correspond to the "meaning" of a verbal statement and the "understanding" of that meaning by another person or persons.* This set is not subject to purely physiological interpretation, since the phenomena entailed *transcend the limits of a single, isolated physiological organism and always involve the interaction of organisms.* This third component of verbal reaction is, thus, *sociological* in character. The formation of verbal meanings requires the establishment of connections among visual, motor, and auditory reactions over the course of long and organized social intercourse between individuals. However, this set, too, is completely objective inasmuch as all the ways and means that serve the formation of verbal connections fall within external apprehension and are on principle accessible to objective methods of study, even if these methods are not purely physiological ones.

The complex apparatus of verbal reactions functions in all its fundamental aspects also when the subject says nothing about his experiences but only undergoes them "in himself," since, if he is conscious of them, a process of *inner* ("covert") speech occurs (we do, after all, think and feel and desire with the help of words; without inner speech we would not become conscious of anything in ourselves). This process of inner speech is just as material as is outward speech.[8]

And so, if in a psychological experiment we replace the subject's "inner experience" with its *verbal equivalent* (inner and outward speech or only inner speech), we still can maintain the integrity and consistency of external, material apprehension. That is how a psychological experiment is viewed by the objectivists.

We have now identified the two trends in modern psychology.

Which of them is in closer correspondence to the basic principles of dialectical materialism? Of course it is the second, the objective trend in psychology. It alone answers the requirements of *materialistic monism.*

Marxism is far from denying the reality of the *subjective-psychical.* Such a thing does exist, to be sure, but under no circumstances can it be divorced from

[8] On verbal reactions, see *ibid.*, Chapter 9, and the article by L. S. Vygotskij, "Soznanie kak problema psixologii povedenija" [Consciousness as a Problem in the Pschology of Behavior], in *Psixologija i Marksizm,* ed. Kornilov (Leningrad, GIZ, 1925).

the *material basis* of the organism's behavior. *The psychical is only one of the properties of organized matter* and, therefore, it does not allow of being placed in opposition to the material, on the order of a special hermeneutical principle. On the contrary, what is essential is to make clear, operating entirely on the grounds of external, material apprehension, under what kind of organization and at what degree of complexity of matter this new quality—the psychical—comes about, it being a property of the very matter itself. Internal, subjective apprehension cannot possibly make the slightest contribution toward that end. In this respect objective psychology is entirely correct.

However, dialectical materialism places still another, very important demand on psychology, a demand by no means always taken into account and implemented by the objectivists: *human* psychology must be *socialized*.

And indeed, is it possible to understand human behavior without bringing to bear an *objective-sociological* point of view? All the fundamental and essential acts in human life are brought about by social stimuli in conditions of a social environment. If we know only the physical component of the stimulus and the abstracted physiological component of the reaction, we still understand exceedingly little about a human act.

To cite an example: The verbal reactions that play so great a role in human behavior (since every single conscious human act is accompanied by inner speech) are not amenable, as we have seen, to purely physiological methods of study; they constitute a specifically *social* manifestation of the human organism.

The formation of verbal reactions is possible only in conditions of a social environment. The complex apparatus of verbal connections is worked and put into practice in a process of long, organized, and multilateral contact among organisms. Psychology cannot, of course, dispense with objective, sociological methods.

In sum, then, psychology must implement *objective methods* and study the *materially expressed behavior of human beings* in conditions of the natural and the *social* environment. Such are the requirements that Marxism makes incumbent upon psychology.

What position does psychoanalysis occupy in the controversy of modern psychological trends?

Freudians, as indeed Freud himself, look upon the Freudian doctrine as the first and only attempt at constructing a truly objective, naturalistic psychology. Russian psychological and philosophical literature, as we pointed out earlier, contains a number of works which try to prove that these claims of psychoanalysis are correct and that in its fundamentals (with, of course, various changes and additions in matters of detail) psychoanalysis best answers the Marxist requirements for a science of psychology.[9] Other representatives of objective psychology

---

[9] A. B. Zalkind, *Frejdizm i marksizm (Očerki kul'tury revoljucionnogo vremeni)* [Freudianism and Marxism (Essays in the Culture of Revolutionary Times)]; an article under

and of Marxism take a different view of psychoanalysis, considering it totally unacceptable from an objective-materialistic point of view.[10]

This issue is an interesting and very important one.

Objective psychology is a young discipline; it is still only beginning to take shape. The way it can best clarify its *point of view* and *methods* is by intelligently criticizing and combating other trends (not to speak, of course, of its direct task of working with the material of behavior). Such efforts will help it become *methodologically* sounder and better able to formulate its position precisely.

Objective psychology is threatened by a certain, quite serious danger—the danger of falling into *naive, mechanistic materialism*. This danger is comparatively mild in those fields of the natural sciences that deal with inorganic nature, but it becomes considerably more serious in biology. *In psychology, a simplistic, mechanistic materialism could well play a disastrous role*. Just such a turn in the direction of primitive materialism and its concomitant *simplification* of the tasks of objective psychology is detectable among the American behaviorists and the Russian reflexologists.

It is precisely when objective psychology confronts the necessity of taking a clearcut critical position with regard to all those complex and extremely important issues raised by psychoanalysis that the insufficiency and crudity of simplistic physiological approaches to human behavior are vividly exposed. At the same time, the necessity of applying a *dialectical and sociological point of view* in psychology becomes manifestly obvious.

The fact is that *critical analysis of Freud's psychological theory will bring us directly in contact with precisely the issue that is of utmost importance and difficulty in human psychology—the issue of verbal reactions and their meaning in human behavior as a whole.*

We shall see that all of the mental phenomena and conflicts that psychoanalysis acquaints us with may be *regarded as complex interrelations and conflicts between the verbal and the nonverbal reactions of humans.*

We shall see that within the verbal domain of human behavior very substantial *conflicts* take place between *inner speech* and *outward speech* and between

---

the same title appeared in *Krasnaja Nov'* 4 (1924); *Žizn' organizma i vnušenie* [The Life of the Organism and the Method of Suggestion] (GIZ, 1927), Chapters 7, 8, and 16. B. Bykovskij, "O metodologičeskix osnovanijax psixoanalitičeskogo učenija Frejda" [On the Methodological Bases of Freud's Psychoanalytical Doctrine], *Pod znamenem Marksizma* 12 (1923). B. D. Fridman, "Osnovnye psixologičeskie vozzrenija Frejda i teorija istoričeskogc materializma" [Freud's Basic Psychological Views and the Theory of Historical Materialism], in Kornilov, *Psixologija i Marksizm*. A. R. Luria, "Psixoanaliz kak sistema monističeskoj psixologii" [Psychoanalysis as a System of Monistic Psychology], in *ibid.*
[10] See V. Jurinec, "Frejdizm i marksizm" [Freudianism and Marxism], *Pod znamenem marksizma* 8-9 (1924), and our article, "Po tu storonu social'nogo" [Beyond the Social], *Zvezda* 5 (1925).

different levels of inner speech. We shall see that the formation of verbal connections (the establishment of connections among visual, motor, and other kinds of reactions over the course of interindividual communication, upon which the formation of verbal reactions depends) proceeds with special difficulty and delay in certain areas of life (for example, the sexual). In the language of Freud, all of this is spoken of as conflicts between the conscious and the unconscious.[11]

Freud's strength lies in his having brought these issues pointedly to the fore and in having gathered the material for their investigation. His weakness lies in his having failed to understand the sociological essence of all these phenomena and in having attempted, instead, to force them into the narrow confines of the individual organism and its psyche. *Processes that are in fact social are treated by Freud from the point of view of individual psychology.*

With this disregard of sociology is coupled another basic deficiency in Freud—the *subjectivity of his method* (granted, a subjectivity somewhat disguised, for which reason it has been a debatable feature). Freud does not consistently and thoroughly maintain the point of view of external, objective apprehension and does attempt to shed light on conflicts in human behavior from within, that is, from the introspective point of view (but again, we repeat, in somewhat disguised form). Thus, his interpretation of the facts and phenomena under his scrutiny is, as we hope to convince the reader, fundamentally unacceptable.

Another problem that arises no less pointedly from a critical evaluation of Freudianism is closely connected with the first problem of verbal reactions. This has to do with the "content of the psyche"—a content consisting of thoughts, desires, dreams, and so forth.[12] This "content of the psyche" is *ideological through and through; from the vaguest of thoughts and dimmest and most uncertain of desires all the way to philosophical systems and complex political institutions, we have one continuous series of ideological and, hence also, sociological phenomena.* Not a single member of this series from one end to the other is the product solely of individual organic creativity. The vaguest of thoughts—even one that remains unarticulated—and a whole complex philosophical movement both equally presuppose organized interindividual communication (allowing, of course, for various kinds and degrees of organization in it). Freud, meanwhile, would have the entire ideological series from one end to the other develop out of the simplest elements of the individual psyche in what amounts to a socially vacuous atmosphere.

---

[11] It should be pointed out that Freud, too, knows a definition of the unconscious as a "non-verbal" entity. Something more on this point will be mentioned later.

[12] Strictly speaking, this is the other side of the same problem since the content of the psyche becomes known to us with the aid of inner speech.

We have here done no more than make preliminary mention of the two cardinal problems in psychology. But we consider it vital that the reader keep these problems constantly in view when following the exposition of psycho-analysis to come.

Now, to conclude this chapter, we must touch upon one other question that we mentioned in passing at the beginning of the chapter.

From what we have already said by way of preliminary orientation, the reader can clearly see that the psychological, that is, the technical-scientific, side of Freudianism is by no means neutral with respect to its general ideological and class position—a position so vividly expressed in its basic philosophical motif.

Not everybody agrees on this point. Many people believe that the *special scientific disciplines* can and should treat their topics in a way completely independent of general world outlook. In the current debate over the object and the methods of study in psychology, certain professionals have advanced the notion of the *higher-level neutrality of the special scientific disciplines, and of psychology among them, in all matters of world outlook and social orientation*.

We believe that that neutrality is a complete fiction. For *sociological* as well as *logical* reasons, such neutrality is impossible.

In point of fact, only if we have not thought through a scientific theory can we fail to notice *its essential connection with basic issues of world outlook*; once we subject it to thoroughgoing scrutiny, any such theory will inevitably reveal a general philosophical orientation.

Thus, subjective psychology in all its various tendencies, provided it follows a consistent development methodologically, inevitably leads to dualism, that is, to the splitting up of being into two incompatible aspects—the material and the mental—or leads to a purely *idealistic* monism. That most seemingly innocent scrap of the "experienced from within," which, as we have seen, undermines the integrity of the objective-material conduct of an experiment in the laboratory, can also serve perfectly well as an Archimedean fulcrum for the break-up of the objective-materialistic picture of the world as a whole.

Scientific neutrality is also impossible in a sociological sense. After all, there is no reason to trust the *subjective sincerity* of human views even at their most earnest. Class interest and presumption constitute an *objective* sociological category of which the *individual* psyche is by no means always aware. But it is precisely *class* interest wherein the power of any theory, of any thought, resides. For indeed, if a thought is powerful, convincing, significant, then obviously it has succeeded in contacting *essential* aspects in the life of the social group in question, succeeded in making a connection between itself and the basic position of that group in the *class struggle*, despite the fact that the creator of that thought might himself be wholly unaware of having done so. The degree of the efficacy and significance of thoughts is directly proportional to their *class-groundedness*, their *ability to be fructified by the socioeconomic being of the group in question.* Let us recall that verbal reactions are a purely social formation. All the enduring, *constant* factors in these reactions are factors precisely of *class*-consciousness and *not of personal* self-conscious.

Human thought never reflects merely the object under scrutiny. It also reflects, along with that object, the being of the scrutinizing subject, his concrete social existence. Thought is a two-sided mirror, and both its sides can and should be clear and unobscured. Exactly what we shall try to do is to understand both sides of Freudian thought.

We have now sufficiently oriented ourselves with respect to basic trends, both in modern philosophy and in modern psychology, and we have acquainted ourselves with the Marxist criteria. We are now equipped with the thread to mark our passage and can plunge ahead into the labyrinth of psychoanalysis.

PART II

AN EXPOSITION
OF FREUDIANISM

CHAPTER 3

The Unconscious and the Dynamics of the Psyche

The conscious and the unconscious. Three periods in the development of Freudianism. The first concept of the unconscious. The method of catharsis. Special features of the first period. The theory of repression.

The human psyche, according to Freud, is divided into three regions: the *conscious*, the *unconscious*, and the *preconscious*. These three regions, or "systems," of the psyche are in a state of incessant interaction, the first two being, additionally, in a state of incessant conflict between themselves. This interaction and this conflict are what the psychical life of human beings amounts to. Each mental act, each manifestation of human behavior, is to be regarded as a *result of the competition and conflict between the conscious and the unconscious—an index of the correlation, reached at a given moment of life, in the power struggle between these two ever-opposing sides.*

Were we to listen only to what the conscious tells us about our mental life, we should never understand that life: The conscious, incessantly struggling with the unconscious, always operates tendentiously. It presents us deliberate falsifications both about itself and about our psychical life in its totality. Yet, psychology had always based its postulates on the evidence of the conscious, and, what is more, the majority of psychologists had simply identified the conscious with the psychical altogether. The few exceptions, such as Lipps and Charcot and his school, who did take the unconscious into account, utterly underestimated its psychical role. They imagined the unconscious to be a kind of absolutely predetermined and stable addendum to mental life. The perpetual dynamics of its conflict with the conscious remained beyond their ken. As a result of this identification of the psychical with consciousness, the older psychology had, in Freud's view, painted a wholly false picture of our psyche, inasmuch as the *primary mass* of the psychical and its *primary centers of power* do in fact fall within the region of the unconscious.

The excitement of Freudianism was the excitement of discovering a whole new world, an unknown continent on the other side of culture and history, but a world that was, at the same time, *extraordinarily close to us,* ready at any moment to erupt through the crust of our consciousness and find reflection in our utterances, our slips of the tongue, our gestures, our behavior.

The proximity of the unconscious and the ease with which it infiltrates the most prosaic matters in life, reaching into the very sum and substance of everyday existence, constitute basic features whereby Freud's theory is distinguished from the doctrines of such high-style "philosophies of the unconscious" as those of Schopenhauer and, especially, Hartmann.

The concept of the unconscious did not acquire instant shape and definition in Freud's mind; it underwent substantial changes as time went on. We see three periods in the history of its development.

In the first period (what might be called the Freud-Breuer period), the Freudian concept of the unconscious was close to the teachings of the eminent French psychiatrists and psychologists Charcot, Lièbault, Bernheim, and Janet. In fact there was direct lineal descent, inasmuch as Freud had studied under Charcot and Bernheim.

The approximate time boundaries of the first period are the years 1890-1897. The basic (and only) book representing that period was Freud and Breuer's *Studien über Hysterie,* which came out in 1895.

During the second, the longest, and the most important period in the development of psychoanalysis, all the basic and characteristic features of the Freudian doctrine on the unconscious took definitive shape. That doctrine became wholly original. All issues during this period were dealt with exclusively *on the level of theoretical and applied psychology.* Freud still avoided making broad philosophical generalizations and dealing with questions of Weltanschauung. The whole idea of the unconscious bore an emphatically *positivistic character.*[1] The style of Freud's works during this period was dry and business-like. The approximate chronological boundaries of this second period are the

---

[1] Even at the present time (1927) Freud still insists upon the strictly empirical nature of his doctrine. According to him, psychoanalysis "is not a philosophical system; it is not derived from a set of rigorously defined premises; it does not aim at encompassing the totality of the world with the aid of those premises; and it does not represent a perfected body of thought that precludes new findings and better reflection." On the contrary, psychoanalysis, he claims, "is based on the facts provided by the field of inquiry, aims at solving the immediate problems that arise from observation . . . , and is always unfinished, always prepared to enter corrections into its theories." *Handwörterbuch der Sexualwissenschaft,* p. 616. [*Editor's note*]

years 1897-1914. During this period all of Freud's basic psychoanalytical works were issued.[2]

In the third, and current, period, the conception of the unconscious has undergone substantial changes (particularly in the works of Freud's students and followers) and has begun to approach the metaphysical doctrines of Schopenhauer and Hartmann. *General issues of Weltanschauung now begin to take precedence over particular, specialized problems.* The unconscious becomes the embodiment of all that belongs both to the lowest and to the highest levels in man (mainly for representatives of the Swiss school of Freudianism). The doctrine on the superego (*Ich-Ideal*) makes its appearance.

How are these changes in the very spirit of the Freudian doctrine to be explained?

The explanation lies partly in the direct influence of Schopenhauer and Hartmann (Nietzsche, as well) whom Freud had begun to study diligently by this time. Previously, throughout the first period and most of the second, Freud, as a consistent positivist, had ignored philosophy.[3] These changes are also partly an expression of the powerful influence of certain of Freud's newer followers who have always been attuned to philosophical and humanistic considerations and who brought this new note into the discussion of psychoanalytical questions (especially Otto Rank and Ferenczi). However, the main role in these changes was most likely played by the reverse influence on Freud of the public whose enthusiasm he had so aroused. Freud, by the time the third period begins, had become an acknowledged "celebrity" for wide circles of the intelligentsia. And these circles had already endeavored to ferret out precisely philosophical, ideological themes, even from Freud's earliest works. They expected and demanded of psychoanalysis, a "revelation" in the domain of Weltanschauung. And so Freud bit by bit succumbed and began to cater to those demands and expectations. What took place is a common enough phenomenon: Success and recognition compromised and somewhat perverted a doctrine that had originally taken shape and had flourished in an atmosphere of hostility and rejection.

The approximate boundary between this third and last period and the second one runs somewhere around 1914-1915.[4] The basic writings of this period are Freud's two most recent books: *Jenseits des Lustprincips* and *Das Ich und das Es*. However, the most striking expression was given this period not in the

---

[2] *Traumdeutung* (1900); *Psychopathologie des Alltagsleben* (1901); *Der Witz* (1905); *Drei Abhandlungen zur Sexualtheorie* (1905). Finally, three basic volumes of the *Kleine Schriften zur Neurosenlehre* and a host of other, lesser works.

[3] See note 1, above.

[4] The first characteristic notes of the last stage of Freudianism began to be struck in such works as *Einführung des Narzissmus* and *Trauer und Melancholie*.

writings of Freud himself but of his favorite student, Otto Rank, whose sensation-producing volume, *The Trauma of Birth*,[5] appeared three years ago (1924). Rank's book is the most characteristic expression of the new spirit that has come to prevail in psychoanalysis today. It is a philosophical tome from start to finish. It is written in the tone and style of a sage "making great and awesome pronouncements." In places it suggests a low-grade parody on the Nietzsche of the Schopenhauer phase.[6] Rank's conclusions are astonishingly extreme. In the dry and sober atmosphere of the second, classical, period of psychoanalysis, such a book would have been a total impossibility.

We have now outlined the three periods in the development of psychoanalysis. The differences and peculiarities of each must always be kept in mind; they cannot be ignored for the sake of constructing a logical unity. Throughout the 33 years of its historical existence psychoanalysis has changed in many and important ways. It no longer is what it was on the eve of World War I.

What is the "unconscious"? How was it first formulated in the earliest period of development of psychoanalysis?

Back in 1889, while he was in Nancy, Freud, then a young Viennese doctor, was extremely impressed with an experiment conducted by the famous expert in hypnosis, Bernheim. A woman patient was hypnotized and instructed to walk to the corner of the room and open an umbrella that was standing there, and to perform these actions at a certain designated time after awakening. Upon awakening and after the designated time period had elapsed, the woman carried out precisely what she had been instructed to do: She walked over to the corner of the room and opened the umbrella in the room. Questioned as to what had made her do that, she responded that she wished to ascertain whether the umbrella was hers. This motive did not in the least correspond to the real reason for the act and obviously had been thought up post factum, but it was perfectly satisfactory for the patient's consciousness: She was sincerely convinced that she had opened the umbrella of her own volition with the aim of determining whether it belonged to her. Later, Bernheim, by persistently questioning the patient and leading her thoughts, finally made her remember the real reason for her act, that is, the instructions she had received under hypnosis.[7]

From this experiment Freud drew three general conclusions that laid the foundations for his earliest conception of the unconscious:

1. *For all its subjective sincerity, the conscious does not always supply a motivation corresponding to the real reasons for an act.*

[5] Trauma der Geburt (1924).
[6] Nietzsche's *Birth of Tragedy*, from which Rank took the epigraph for his book.
[7] See Freud, "Zur Geschichte der psychoanalytischen Bewegung," in *Kleine Schriften zur Neurosenlehre*, Part 4.

2. An act can sometimes be determined by forces that operate in the psyche but do not reach the conscious.
3. With the help of certain techniques, these psychical forces can be brought to consciousness.

On the basis of these propositions, which were verified by his own psychiatric practice, Freud, in collaboration with his older colleague, Breuer, worked out what was called the "cathartic method of treating hysteria."[8]

The gist of this method consists in the following. At the basis of hysteria and other *psychogenic* nervous disorders lie psychical complexes submerged below the conscious of the patient. Involved here are various possible mental disturbances, feelings, or desires that the patient had once experienced but then had *deliberately forgotten* because his conscious, for one reason or another, was afraid or ashamed of remembering them. Without surfacing in the conscious, these forgotten experiences cannot be "lived out" and "worked through" (or "discharged") in the normal way. Just such experiences cause the pathological symptoms of hysteria. The doctor's efforts are supposed to remove the *amnesia* in which these experiences are held, to bring them to the patient's conscious, to integrate them with that conscious and thereby make it possible for these experiences to be lived out and discharged without hindrance. By means of such a process of "living out" the pathological symptoms of hysteria are done away with.

To take a hypothetical example: A young lady feels toward a closely related person a kind of attraction, which from her own point of view seems so inadmissible, so bizarre, so unnatural that she cannot acknowledge that feeling even to herself. Therefore, she is in no position to subject that feeling to responsible and conscious discussion even in private with herself. Such an experience, which she herself cannot acknowledge, will assume in the young lady's psyche a completely *isolated status*; it will not be able to enter into any connection with other experiences, thoughts, considerations. Fear, shame, and indignation will drive that experience into severe mental exile. In its isolated state, this experience cannot find a way out of exile, since the normal outlet would be some kind of action, some form of behavior, or, at least, the discourse and reasoned arguments of consciousness. But all such outlets are closed. The isolated experience, hemmed in on all sides (or "bracketed"—*eingeklemmte*, as Freud puts it), begins to seek an outlet along abnormal routes where it might remain unrecognized—for example, in the paralysis of some perfectly healthy limb, in causeless outbreaks of terror, in some kind of nonsensical activity, and so on. Thereby the symptoms of hysteria take shape. The doctor's task in the

---

[8] For all that follows here, see Freud and Breuer, *Studien über Hysterie*, 1st edition [1895]; 4th edition [1922] or the article by Freud in *Handwörterbuch*, p. 160.

given instance amounts primarily to discovering from the patient the reason for her illness, a reason she has forgotten and cannot acknowledge, and forcing her to call it to mind. (For this purpose, Freud and Breuer used either full or partial hypnosis.) Once having discovered the reason for the illness, the doctor must force the patient, while helping her overcome her fear and shame, to stop "camouflaging" it in hysterical symptoms and to engage it into the "normal workings" of her consciousness. In doing this, the doctor makes it possible for the experience to discharge normally, either by way of conscious struggle with it or, at times, by way of expedient concessions to it. Perhaps our young lady patient will have to contend with severe adversity or embarrassments in her life, but she will no longer have to contend with illness. The hysterical symptoms will become superfluous and gradually will cease.

To this liberation from a fearful and shameful experience via the "living out" of the experience Freud applied the Aristotelean term "catharsis" (in Aristotle's theory of poetics, tragedy purges the spectators' souls of the effects of pity and terror by making the spectators experience these feelings in diluted form). Hence the name given by Freud and Breuer to their method—the "cathartic method."

The "unconscious," as Freud understood it in the first period of development of his doctrine, was comprised of just such forgotten experiences that caused symptoms of hysteria. This version of the unconscious defined it as a sort of *foreign body* that penetrated into the psyche. Such a foreign body did not have firm associational bonds with other factors in the psyche and thus disrupted its integrity. A close counterpart in normal life was the state of daydreaming, since it, too, was freer of the tight associational bonds that infiltrate our consciousness than were real-life experiences. Another close counterpart was the hypnotic state, for which reason Freud and Breur called the unconscious the "hypnoid."

Such was Freud's earliest conception of the unconscious.

Let us now note and underscore two special features of it. First, Freud did not provide us any physiological theory of the unconscious, nor did he make any attempt to do so—in contrast to Breuer, who did propose physiological substantiation for his method. Freud, on the contrary, *turned his back on physiology from the very start*. Second, the products of the unconscious were obtainable only *in translation into the language of consciousness*: There was no direct access possible to the unconscious other than the conscious of the patient himself.

We must once again point out to the reader the enormous importance that the cathartic method attached to *verbal reactions*. Freud himself made explicit reference to this feature of his theory: He compared his method of treating hysteria with the confession in the Catholic church. At confession, a believer really does obtain relief and purification thanks to his telling another person, in this case, the priest, about thoughts and acts that he himself considers sinful and that he could not, under other circumstances, have told to anyone. In this way he gives *verbal expression* and *verbal outlet* to what was bottled up inside and isolated in his psyche and had been oppressing it. Therein lies the cleansing power of speech.[9]

Now we must proceed to the further development of the concept of the unconscious that took place in the second, classical, period of psychoanalysis. Here, the concept of the unconscious became enriched with a host of new and most vital factors.

During the first period, the unconscious had been conceived of, to a certain degree, as an *incidental phenomenon* in the human psyche—a sort of pathological addendum, a foreign body that had penetrated the psyche of an hysterically inclined person under the influence of chance circumstances in that person's life. The normal psychical apparatus was conceived of, during the same period, as something entirely static and steadfast. *The conflict of psychical forces was not at all regarded as a constant and regular form of mental life* but, rather, as an *exceptional and abnormal occurrence in it.* Moreover, the content of the unconscious remained entirely unelucidated and also seems to have been regarded as fortuitous. Depending on a person's individual characteristics and on chance circumstances in his life, some painful or shameful experience is isolated, and forgotten and becomes unconscious. No *typological generalizations* about such experiences were made by Freud. The exceptional significance of the sexual factor had not yet been advanced. Such was the state of affairs during the first period.

Now, in the second period, the unconscious becomes an essential and extremely vital component of the psychical apparatus of every single human being. The very psychical apparatus itself becomes *dynamic,* that is, is set into perpetual motion. The conflict between the conscious and the unconscious is declared a constant and regular form of psychical life. The unconscious, moreover, becomes a productive source of psychical forces and energies for all domains of cultural creativity, especially for art. At the same time, the unconscious can become the source of all nervous disorders whenever its conflict with the conscious goes awry.

According to these new views of Freud's, the process of formation of the unconscious is a perfectly regular phenomenon and takes place throughout a person's life, starting from the very moment of birth. The process itself is termed "repression" (*Verdrängung*). Repression is one of the most important concepts of the entire psychoanalytical doctrine. Furthermore, during this same period,

---

[9] It should be noted that Freud, in this same period, had stopped using hypnosis for cathartic purposes in his own psychiatric practice and had replaced it with the method of free association. By persistent questioning and long observation the doctor, having first prepared the patient, explores for those "shameful and fearful" experiences that have been driven deep into the unconscious and, finding them, brings them to the patient's consciousness where they are able to discharge naturally. [*Editor's note*]

the content of the unconscious is typologized: No longer does that content consist of incidental and arbitrary experiences but, rather, of certain bound sets of experiences (complexes) that are typical for and fundamentally *common* to all human beings and bear a specific—primarily sexual—character. These *complexes* are repressed into the unconscious *at certain strictly defined periods* that occur and recur throughout the history of the life of every human being.

In the present chapter, we shall familiarize ourselves with the basic psychical "mechanism" of repression and the concept of "censorship" closely associated with it. The content of the unconscious we shall leave for the following chapter.

What is repression?

In the early stages of the development of the human personality, our psyche knows no distinction between the possible and the impossible, the beneficial and the harmful, the permissible and the forbidden. It is governed by one principle alone—the "pleasure principle" (*Lustprincip*).[10] At the dawn of the development of the human soul, free and unhampered play is enjoyed by notions, feelings, desires that at later stages of development would horrify the conscious. In the child's soul "all is permitted." There are for it no immoral feelings and desires, and, not knowing fear or shame, it makes broad use of this privilege, accumulating a huge store of the most depraved images, feelings, and desires— "depraved" from the point of view of later stages of development, needless to say. To this unbounded domination of the pleasure principle is joined, at the very earliest stage of development, the ability to achieve *hallucinatory satisfaction of desires*, seeing that an infant cannot yet tell the difference between what is real and what is not. For an infant, a mental representation is already the real thing. Hallucinatory satisfaction of desires (wish fulfillment) is retained by human beings throughout life in dreams.[11]

At later stages of development, the pleasure principle relinquishes its exclusive hold over the psyche; along with it—often in spite of it—a new principle of psychical life begins to operate. This is the "reality principle." All psychical events must now pass a *double examination* from the viewpoints of both these principles. Indeed, a desire may turn out to be unsatisfiable and therefore a cause of suffering or a desire, once satisfied, may bring on disagreeable consequences. Such desires must be suppressed. A mental presentation may be closely linked by association with feelings of fear or remembrances of pain. Such images must be kept from emerging in the psyche.

Thus, a process of psychical selection comes about, and only mental formations that pass the twofold test from the viewpoints of both principles are legitimized and enfranchised, so to speak, and either enter into the higher system

[10] Freud, "Über zwei Princip des psychologischen Geschehens," in *Kleine Schriften zur Neurosenlehre*, Part 3, p. 271.

[11] See *Traumdeutung*.

of the psyche—the *conscious*—or acquire the possibility of doing so, thus becoming the *preconscious*. Meanwhile, experiences that do not pass the test become illegitimate and are repressed into the system of the *unconscious*.

This repression is accomplished *automatically, without any participation of the conscious*, and operates this way throughout a person's entire life. The conscious comes into being fully-fledged and purified; items that have been repressed do not register in the conscious and it may totally lack the slightest inkling of their presence or makeup. What takes charge of repression is another, special psychical force that Freud picturesquely termed the "censorship." The censorship occupies a position on the border between the systems of the unconscious and the conscious. Everything that has come into the conscious, or has the possibility of doing so, has undergone a rigorous process of censorship.[12]

The entire mass of "uncensored" presentations, feeling and desires repressed into the unconscious *never expires* and never loses its power. Indeed, a feeling or desire can only be "lived out" and gotten rid of through the conscious and through the actions and behavior it controls—above all, human speech. The unconscious is nonverbal, it abhors words. We cannot acknowledge our unconscious desires even to ourselves in inner speech. Consequently, these desires have no way out; they cannot be worked through, and, therefore, they go on living in our psyche with their full power and vitality unimpaired.[13]

Such is the way the process of repression works.

We can now define the unconscious, in terms of the *psychical dynamics* of its formation, as *the repressed*. What character the repressed bears or, in other words, what its content is, we shall elucidate in the next chapter.

---

[12] On this point, in addition to *Traumdeutung*, see *Das Ich und das Es*, Chapters 1 and 2.

[13] *Jenseits des Lustprincips*, pp. 35-36; and *Kleine Schriften zur Neurosenlehre*, Part 4: "Das Unbewusste."

CHAPTER 4

The Content of
the Unconscious

The theory of instincts. The sexual life of the child. The Oedipus Complex. The content of the unconscious in the second period of Freudianism. The theory of instincts in the third period (Eros and Death). The Super-ego.

We are now acquainted with the operation of repression. The next question is: Where does the material for repression come from?

Exactly what kind of feelings, desires, mental presentations are repressed into the unconscious?

In order to understand what is at issue here—that is, in order to be able to deal with the content of the unconscious—we must familiarize ourselves with Freud's *theory of instincts* (*Triebe*).[1]

Psychical activity is set in motion by *external and internal stimuli* on the organism. Internal stimuli have a somatic source, that is, they originate within our organism. The psychical counterparts of these internal, somatic *stimuli* are what Freud calls the *instincts*.

Freud divides all instincts into two sets according to their aims and somatic source:

1. *Sexual instincts, the aim of which is the continuation of the species even at the cost of the individual's life;*

2. *Personal or ego instincts (Ich-triebe), the aim of which is individual self-preservation.*

Neither of these two sets is reducible to the other, and they often enter into mutual conflicts of various kinds.

---

[1] "Triebe und Triebschicksale," in *Kleine Schriften zur Neurosenlehre; Das Ich und das Es,* Chapter 4.

Here we shall be concerned only with the sexual instincts, since they provide the main bulk of the material for the unconscious. This set of instincts has been thoroughly investigated by Freud.[2] A number of people maintain that the chief merits of Freudianism lie precisely in the domain of sexual theory.

We mentioned in the preceding chapter that the child, at the earliest stages of his psychical life, amasses an enormous store of feelings and desires that are depraved and immoral from the point of view of the conscious. To the reader unacquainted with Freud that assertion no doubt seemed very odd and possibly even caused some perplexity. Indeed, where in the world does a child get immoral, depraved desires? A child, after all, is the very symbol of innocence and purity!

The sexual instinct or, to use another Freudian term, the *libido* is inherent in the child from the very start of his life; it originates with the birth of his body and carries on a permanent existence in his organism and psyche, an existence that may from time to time lose force but never is altogether extinguished. Sexual maturity is only one stage—granted, a stage of great importance—in the development of sexuality but by no means its point of origin.

During those early stages of development wherein the pleasure principle, with its "all is permitted," reigns supreme, the sexual instinct has the following distinguishing characteristics:

1. The genitals have not yet become the somatic organizing center of the sexual instinct; they are only one set of so-called "erogenous zones" and are in equal competition with other zones of the body such as, for example, the oral cavity (in the act of sucking), the anus or anal zone (in the act of defecating), the skin, the thumb, the big toe, and the like. It could be claimed that the sexual instinct, or libido, of the child, before it can focus and concentrate in the as yet immature sexual organs, is diffused throughout the child's body, so that any part of that body whatsoever is capable of becoming a somatic source of sexual arousal. In view of the fact that at this stage the sexual organs, the genitals, have not yet become the body's center for the sexual instinct, Freud has named it the "pregenital stage." It should be noted that a certain degree of sexual arousal still remains possible for the erogenous zones (especially the mouth and the anus) throughout the entire remainder of a person's life.[3]

---

[2] For the exposition that follows, see Freud, *Drei Abhandlungen zur Sexualtheorie* (1905).

[3] The development of the sexual instinct in the child passes through the following stages, according to Freud: The first pregenital stage is the oral stage, wherein the mouth plays the principal role, in compliance with the child's most essential interests; the next stage is the anal stage; finally, the last stage is reached when the genital zone occupies the prime position. In Freud's view, the child passes through all these stages quite rapidly—within the course of four to five years after birth. [*Editor's note*]

2. A child's sexual instinct is *not yet autonomous or differentiated*; it joins in closely with other needs of the organism and the processes of their satisfaction—the processes of eating, suckling, urination, defecation, and others, thereby imbuing all these other processes with a *sexual coloration*.

3. A child's sexual instinct in its first, "oral" stage can be satisfied *by his own body* without need for an *object* (another person). *The child*, therefore, *is autoerotic*.

4. Since the primacy of the genitals, their predominance in sexual life, has not yet been established, the sexual discrimination of the child is in an ambiguous state. It can be claimed, then, that in its earliest development the sexual instinct is *bisexual*.

5. As a result of all these features in the early development of the sexual instinct, the child is a *polymorph pervers*: He is susceptible to masochism, sadism, homosexuality, and other perversions. This is a natural consequence of the fact that his libido is diffused throughout his body and can join with any process or organic sensation, deriving sexual pleasure from it. What the child is least able to understand is precisely the normal sex act. As regards the sexual perversions of adults, Freud considers them a phenomenon of *retarded normal development*, a regression to earlier stages of infantile sexuality.

Such are, according to Freud, the main features of infantile eroticism.

We can now more clearly appreciate the huge store of sexual desires, and the images and feelings connected with them, that can come about in a child's psyche, grounded in the infantile libido, and must afterward be mercilessly repressed into the unconscious.

We may say that the entire early period in the history of our psyche takes place outside the boundaries of consciousness—indeed, rarely do people recall what happened to them before the age of four. Nevertheless, the events of that period do not lose their power but remain alive in our unconscious; this is "past history" that has not died but perseveres in the present inasmuch as it has not been "lived out."

The most important event in the repressed history of infantile sexual life is the child's *sexual attraction to his mother* and, coupled with it, *hatred for his father*—the so-called *Oedipus complex*.[4] The doctrine on this complex and its role in human life is one of the most crucial points in Freudianism. The gist of it amounts to the following. The first object of a human being's sexual instinct—*sexual* in the sense of infantile eroticism as characterized above—is his *mother*. A child's relationship with his mother is acutely *sexualized* from the very start. According to Otto Rank, the authoritative disciple of Freud whom we have

---

[4] On this, see Freud, *Traumdeutung*; Jung, *Die Bedeutung des Vaters für das Schiksal des Einzelnen*; and O. Rank, *Incestmotiv in Dichtung und Sage* and *Trauma der Geburt*.

already mentioned, even the time the foetus spends in its mother's womb has a libidinous character, and it is actually with the event of birth—the first and most distressing separation from the mother, the rupture of unity with her—that the Oedipus tragedy begins.[5] The libido, however, continues time and time again to be impelled toward the mother, sexualizing all her attentions and services; the activities of being nursed, being bathed, being helped with defecation, and so forth acquire a sexual coloration for the child. Here, too, are involved inevitable contacts with the various erogenous zones and the genitals that cause the child to experience pleasurable feelings and even sometimes his first erection. The child is drawn to his mother's bed, clings to his mother's body, and some obscure memory in his organism impels him to his mother's uterus, to return to that uterus. In this way the child is *organically* impelled toward *incest*. The situation is such that incestuous desires, feelings, and presentations are inevitably bound to arise.

In the course of these attractions of the little Oedipus to his mother, the *father* becomes the rival who incurs the hatred of his son. The father, after all, interferes with the child's relationship with his mother: He keeps the child from being taken into her bed, he forces the child to be self-reliant, to do without his mother's help, and so on. From this arises the child's infantile wish for the father's death, a death that would allow him to take undivided possession of the mother. Since the pleasure principle reigns supreme in the child's psyche at this stage of development, there is no limit to the production of both *incestuous* and *hostile* tendencies and desires and the images associated with them.[6]

When the reality principle comes into force and the father's voice, with all its prohibitions, begins gradually to transform into the voice of the child's own conscience, an onerous and relentless struggle with these incestuous impulses begins and they are repressed into the unconscious. The entire Oedipus complex is subjected to full amnesia. *Fear and shame* are engendered in place of the repressed impulses; they are brought about in the psyche by the very idea of the possibility of sexual impulses toward one's mother. The censorship has done a splendid job: The legal—the "official"—conscious protests with complete sincerity against the mere suggestion of the possibility of the Oedipus complex.

The Oedipus complex, according to Freud, does not by any means always pass through the process of repression without painful consequences for the child. It frequently leads to nervous disorders, in particular various infantile phobias.[7]

For Freud the concept of the Oedipus complex makes fully comprehensible why *myths* about incest, about the murder of a father by his son or, conversely,

---

[5] Rank, *Trauma der Geburt*.

[6] The same is applicable, with relations reversed, to a female child.

[7] See Freud, "Geschichte der Fobie eines 5-jährigen Knaben," in *Kleine Schriften zur Neurosenlehre*, Part 3.

about a father murdering his children, and other related legends are so wide-spread among so many different peoples. It also explains the overwhelming impression that Sophocles' famous tragedy makes on all of us, despite the fact that, from the point of view of the official conscious, we are bound to regard the Oedipus plot as a poetic fiction and a situation not in the least *typical* of human life. But this tragedy, Freud maintains, just as *any other great work of art, appeals not to our official conscious but to the whole of our psyche, above all, to the deepest levels of our unconscious.*[8]

The Oedipus complex, this first, prehistoric event in human life, has, according to Freud's theory, enormous, direct, and decisive significance for that life. This first love and first hate will always remain the most integrally organic feelings in a man's life. In comparison with these feelings all subsequent erotic relations, relations occurring in the light of consciousness, will amount to superficial and cerebral experiences, experiences that do not engage *the very depths of the organism and the psyche.* Rank and Ferenczi outrightly consider all of a man's subsequent love relations only a surrogate for his first, Oedipal love—a love that had been preceded by complete organic unity with its object, the mother. Future coitus is only a partial compensation for the lost paradise of the intrauterine state. All events in adult life borrow their psychical power from this first event that has been repressed into the unconscious—the Oedipus complex. In his later life a man will, without of course being in the least aware of it himself, reenact this aboriginal event of the Oedipus complex time and time again with the new partners in his life, transferring to them his repressed and, hence, eternally alive feelings toward his mother and father. The basis for this process is the so-called transference mechanism (*Übertragung*).

The transference mechanism is a very important point in psychoanalytical theory and practice. Freud understands it as *the unconscious displacement of repressed instincts*—principally sexual—*from their direct object to another, substitute object.* So, for example, during psychoanalytical treatment, the patient's attraction to his mother and enmity toward his father are usually transferred to the doctor, and in this way they are partially lived out. Therein lies the significance of transference for the practice of psychotherapy. Transference is one of the ways of *bypassing* the prohibitions of the official conscious and, even if only partially, of giving the unconscious a chance to come into its own and express itself.

Freud maintains that a man's love life depends in many respects on the degree of his success in freeing his libido from its attraction to his mother. *The first object of juvenile infatuation usually resembles the mother.*

---

[8] Psychological investigations of the type that use a psychoanalytical base in the endeavor to penetrate the depths of the human psyche (the region of the unconscious) have acquired in psychoanalytical literature the new term "depth psychology" (*Tiefenpsychologie*). [*Editor's note*]

However, the image of the mother may also play a disastrous role in the development of the sexual instinct. Fear of incest can, for the official conscious, render love of mother into an expressly spiritual kind of love—so-called respectful love—which is incompatible with even the idea of sensuality, and this fear can, moreover, form bonds in a man's psyche with any kind of respect, any kind of spirituality. Often this makes sexual intercourse with a woman one loves and respects impossible and leads to a fatal split of the unitary sexual instinct into two separate currents—sensual passion and spiritual attachment—which cannot join together in one and the same object.[9]

The Oedipus complex and everything associated with it comprise the main content of the unconscious system. Other, lesser sets of repressed psychical formations tie into the Oedipus complex throughout the entire course of a person's life. Culture and the individual's cultural growth require ever fresher repressions. But on the whole, *the bulk, the so-to-speak basic fund of the unconscious is comprised of infantile impulses that are sexual in character.* Of the "ego instincts," mention need be made only of the so-called *aggressive* impulses. In the infantile psyche, with its "all is permitted," these aggressive impulses appear full-blown: A child rarely wishes his enemies anything less than death. Such "mental murders" of persons, including even those closest to the child, amass in quantity during the first years of the child's life. They are all repressed into the unconscious later on. Owing to the predominance of the pleasure principle, the child is in all respects a pure and thoroughgoing egotist. This egotism knows no bounds, whether moral or cultural. A fair amount of material for the unconscious is produced on these grounds, as well.

Such, in terms of basic features, is the content of the unconscious. It can be summed up in the following formulaic statement: The world of the unconscious takes in everything that the organism might have done, had it been given over to the pleasure principle pure and simple and not been bound by the reality principle and culture. Thus, into the unconscious passes everything the organism really desired and had vivid presentations of (but satisfied to an insignficant degree) in the earliest, infantile stage of life when the pressure of the reality principle and of culture was still weak and when, moreover, the manifestations of a human's innate, organic self-centeredness were freer.

All of the above definitions and characterizations of the basic factors in Freud's conception of the unconscious—the pleasure and reality principles, repression, censorship, the theory of instincts, and, finally, the content of the unconscious—were worked out by Freud, as already noted, during the second and most positive period in the development of psychoanalysis. We in fact relied primarily on the works of that period for our exposition.

---

[9] Freud, "Zur Psychologie des Liebesleben," in *Kleine Schrifter zur Neurosenlehre*, Part 4.

However, we know that this theory of Freud's underwent quite substantial changes and expansions in the third period of development. We are also aware of the direction these changes took.

We shall not stop to consider in detail the whole set of new features that the third period brought in. After all, the culmination point of its development is in the offing only now, at the very time this is being written. Meanwhile, there is quite a lot about this period that has not yet taken definitive shape or reached final resolution. Both of Freud's books especially characteristic of this period suffer from inconclusiveness and, here and there, obscurity, differing in these respects from the almost classical lucidity, precision, and definitiveness of his earlier works. Therefore, we shall limit ourselves to a brief review of only what is of greatest importance.

The theory of instincts has undergone substantial changes. Instead of the earlier division into sexual instincts (continuation of the species) and ego instincts (preservation of the individual), a new binary division has appeared: (1) the *sexual instinct, or Eros,* and (2) *the death instinct.* The ego instinct, above all the idea of self-preservation, has been consigned to the sexual instinct (Eros), which thus has undergone considerable conceptual expansion, encompassing both sections of the earlier division.

By *Eros* Freud means the *instinct striving toward organic life,* toward its preservation and development at whatever cost, whether in terms of the continuation of the species (sexuality in the narrow sense) or preservation of the individual. *The death instinct* is understood as *aiming toward the return of all living organisms to the lifeless state of inorganic, inanimate matter*—a striving away from the exigencies of life and Eros.

All life, Freud maintains, is conflict and compromise between these two strivings. Every cell of a living organism contains the combination of both kinds of instincts—Eros and Death; to the one and the other, respectively, correspond the physiological processes of construction (anabolism) and destruction (catabolism) of living matter. As long as a cell is alive, Eros is dominant.

When the restless, life-oriented Eros finds satisfaction in the sexual way, then Death begins to make itself heard. Hence, the resemblance between the postcoital state and dying, and for certain lower animals the coincidence of the act of fertilization with actual death. The latter die because, once Eros is stilled, the death instinct is completely free to operate and carries out its task.

In its biological aspect, this new theory of Freud's reflects the strong influence of the noted German biologist and neo-Darwinian, Weismann; in its philosophical aspect, the equally strong influence of Schopenhauer.

The second special feature of the third period of development that we shall deal with is the expansion of the content of the unconscious, its enrichment with qualitatively new and unique factors.

A dynamic conception of the unconscious as "the repressed" was characteristic of the second period. Freud dealt with that conception primarily in his psychiatric research,[10] and, indeed, technical psychiatric interests were predominant during that period. The repressed, consisting, as we have seen, largely of sexual instincts, was regarded as antagonistic toward the conscious "I"—the ego. Now, in his most recent book, Freud proposes that the whole region of the psyche not coinciding with the ego be called *"das Es"*—"the id." The id is that inner, shadowy, elemental force made up of appetites and impulses that we do sometimes very keenly feel within us and that stands in opposition to our rational persuasions and good will. The id is the passions; the ego, the intelligence and reason. In the id the pleasure principle reigns supreme; the ego is the vehicle for the reality principle. The id is, moreover, unconscious.

Up to now, when speaking of the unconscious, we have had to do exclusively with the id—repressed impulses are, after all, precisely its properties. Therefore, the entire unconscious had the appearance of something *lower*, something *dark and immoral*, whereas everything higher, moral, and rational coincided with the conscious. This view is invalid. It is not only the id that is unconscious. The ego, too, and the ego *in its highest sphere*, accommodates *a region of the unconscious*.

In point of fact, the process of repression, which issues from the ego, is unconscious, and the work of the censorship, which is carried out in the interests of the ego, is likewise unconscious. Thus, a significant area of the ego also turns out to be unconscious. This is the area on which Freud has focused his attention during the third period. It was discovered to be far broader, deeper, and more substantial than it had seemed at first. From what we know of the unconscious as the repressed, we might conclude that *a normal human being is far more immoral than he himself believes*. This conclusion is correct, but we must now add that the normal human being is also *far more moral than he knows*. "Human nature," Freud writes, "has a far greater extent, both for good and for evil, than it thinks it has—i.e., than its ego is aware of through conscious perception."[11]

This higher, unconscious region in the ego Freud termed the *superego* (*Ich-ideal*).

The superego is first and foremost that *censor* whose orders are carried out by the process of repression. Moreover, the superego makes its presence felt in a whole host of other very important phenomena of personal and cultural life. It comes out in an *unaccountable sense of guilt* that oppresses the minds of certain people. The conscious does not acknowledge this guilt; it struggles with the

---

[10] "Pathological research has directed our interest too exclusively to the repressed," Freud himself remarks in *Das Ich und das Es*. [English translation from *The Standard Edition of the Complete Psychological Works of Sigmund Freud* (hereafter cited as *Standard Edition*), ed. James Strachey (London: The Hogarth Press and the Institute of Psycho-Analysis, 24 volumes, 1953-1974), 19 (1961): 19. *Translator.*]

[11] *Standard Edition* 19:52.

feelings aroused but cannot overcome them. These feelings have played a major role in various manifestations of religious atrocities connected with the affliction of suffering on oneself (asceticism, self-flagellation, self-immolation and the like). Furthermore, among manifestations of the superego belong "sudden instigations of conscience," instances of unusual severity toward one's own self, self-contempt, melancholy, and so forth. In all these phenomena the conscious "I"—the ego—is compelled to submit to a force *emanating from the depths of the unconscious, but a force that is, at the same time, moral*, often even "hypermoral," to use Freud's own term.

How was that force formed in the human psyche? How did the superego come about?

To understand this requires acquainting ourselves with a special psychical mechanism called "identification." A person's attraction to another person may go in either of two directions: It may aim at possessing that other person (for example, the child during the Oedipal phase strives to possess his mother), but it may also cause the person to strive to identify himself with the other, to conform to him, to become just like him, to assimilate that other person into his self. This second tendency is precisely the child's attitude toward his father—he wants to be like his father, to copy him. This second kind of relationship to an object (person) outside oneself is, moreover, the older of the two; it is connected with the earliest, oral stage of child development and the development of the human species. In this phase, the child—and prehistoric man—knows no other way of approach to an object than to ingest it; whatever seems to him of value he immediately tries to put into his mouth and, in that way, introduce into his organism. The endeavor to imitate is, as it were, the psychical surrogate for the more ancient ingestion. In human life, identification sometimes replaces the normal endeavor to possess the object of one's love. So, for example, in a case of unsuccessful love, where possession of the love object is impossible, a person may assimilate the qualities of the loved one, become like and identify with the loved one.[12] *Identification also explains the emergence of the superego in the human psyche.*

Of greatest importance for the formation of the superego is identification with the father during the period of the Oedipus complex. Here the child assimilates the image of his father, including the latter's virility, threats, commands, prohibitions. From this originate the superego's harsh and severe tones, expressed in the commands of conscience, of duty, of the categorical imperative, and so on. "You must . . . !" first rings in a person's soul as the voice of the father of the Oedipus complex stage; it is repressed together with the Oedipus complex into the unconscious, from where it continues to make itself heard as the voice of inner authority, of duty, of the highest commands of conscience,

[12] See Freud, *Massenpsychologie und Ich-Analyse* (1921), pp. 68-77.

entirely independent of the ego. Later in life, the authority of teachers, of religion, of culture are added to the father's voice, but these influences are more superficial and conscious and, therefore, must themselves borrow power from the earlier self-identification of a person with his father and with his father's will. "The superego," Freud writes, "retains the character of the father, while the more powerful the Oedipus complex was and the more rapidly it succumbed to repression, the stricter will be the domination of the superego over the ego later on—in the form of conscience or perhaps of an unconscious sense of guilt."[13]

Such is Freud's doctrine on the superego.

In concluding this chapter, let us note that in his latest book Freud defines the unconscious as *nonverbal*; it converts into the preconscious (from which it can always proceed into the conscious) "through becoming connected with the word presentations corresponding to it."[14] Freud ascribes greater significance to this definition here than he had done in his earlier works. Nevertheless, even here it remains without further elaboration.

With this we conclude our characterization of the unconscious. We now know its origins and we know its content, but we still do not know the most important of all—what was the material and what were the methods, that is, the investigatory procedures, that Freud used in order to arrive at all this knowledge about the unconscious? Only the answer to that question can, after all, put us in a position to judge the scientific validity and reliability of all that knowledge. To that topic the next chapter is devoted.

[13] *Standard Edition* 19:34-35.
[14] There, too, Freud cites the earlier work where that definition was first given. [See *Standard Edition* 19:20. *Translator.*]

CHAPTER 5

The Psychoanalytical Method

Compromise formations. The method of free association. Interpretation of dreams. Neurotic symptoms. The psychopathology of everyday life.

When expositing the early Freudian concept of the unconscious, we emphasized that Freud had not found *direct and unmediated* access to the unconscious but had learned about it *through the conscious* of the patient himself. Exactly the same thing has to be said about his mature method. Indeed, here is what Freud himself says on this point in his latest book: "All our knowledge is invariably bound up with consciousness. We can come to know the unconscious only by making it conscious."[1]

Freud's *psychological method* boils down to an *interpretative analysis* of *conscious formations* of a special kind—ones that *allow of being traced back to their unconscious roots.*

What are these formations like?

As we already know, the unconscious is precluded from direct access to the conscious and to the preconscious, at the threshold of which the censorship operates. However, as we also know, all repressed impulses retain their energy and, therefore, constantly strive to break through into consciousness.

They can do this (only partially) with the help of *compromises and distortions* that deceive the censorship and circumvent its vigilance. This distortion and disguising of repressed impulses occurs, of course, in the region of the unconscious, and it is from there, once having deceived the censorship, that they penetrate into the conscious, where they remain unrecognized. It is here, in the conscious, that the investigator finds them and subjects them to analysis.

---

[1] *Standard Edition* 19·19.

All these compromise formations fall into one or the other of two sets:

1. *Pathological formations*—symptoms of hysteria, obsessions, phobias, and also such pathological phenomena of everyday life as the forgetting of names, slips of the tongue and pen, and the like;

2. *Normal formations*—dreams, myths, and the images of creative art, philosophical, social, and even political ideas, in fact, the whole domain of human *ideological creativity*.

The border between these two sets is fluid, so that it is often difficult to tell where the normal ends and the pathological begins.

Freud's most substantive research was devoted to *dreams*. The methods of interpretation he applied to dream imagery have become classical and standard procedures for psychoanalysis as a whole.

Freud distinguishes two factors in a dream: (1) its manifest content (*manifester Inhalt*)—the dream images, usually taken from random impressions of the immediately preceding day, that we easily remember and willingly speak about with other people; and (2) latent dream thoughts (*latente Traumgedanken*) that fear the light of consciousness and are artfully *disguised* in the images of the manifest content of the dream. The conscious often does not even suspect their existence.[2]

How does one delve down to those latent thoughts, that is, how does one *interpret* dreams?

For this purpose, Freud proposed the method of "free fantasizing" (*freie Einfälle*) or "free association" (*freie Assoziation*) apropos the manifest images of the dream under scrutiny. *Free rein must be given to the psyche and all the restraining and critical faculties of consciousness must be relaxed*; one must allow anything at all to come to mind, even the most outlandish thoughts and images that have no apparent relevance to the dream being analyzed; one must become completely *passive* and allow free access to whatever comes to consciousness, even if it seem senseless, meaningless, with no connection to the matter at hand; one must endeavor only to be attentive to whatever *involuntarily* arises in the psyche.

When we actually attempt to do this, we immediately become aware that our efforts meet with strong *resistance* on the part of our conscious; a kind of *inner protest* is generated against our interpreting our dream. This protest takes various forms: Now we feel that the manifest content of the dream is understandable enough as is and needs no explanation; now, on the contrary, we regard our dream as so absurd and ridiculous that it cannot possibly make any sense; finally, we take a critical attitude toward the thoughts and images that

---

[2] Freud, *Traumdeutung*. The latter are sometimes called "residues of the day" because of their relation with impressions while awake.

enter our mind and we suppress them the instant they arise as things accidental and unrelated to the dream. In other words, *we constantly strive to maintain and adhere to the point of view of the legal conscious*; we are reluctant to overstep the laws that govern the territory of our psyche's highest level.

In order to *delve into the latent thoughts* of a dream, *this stubborn resistance must be overcome*. It, this resistance, represents precisely that force which, in the capacity of the censorship, has distorted the true content (the latent thoughts) of our dream and transformed it into the dream's manifest images (manifest content). This force is what hampers our present efforts; it is the cause of our easily and rapidly forgetting dreams and is responsible for those involuntary distortions to which we subject dreams when we do remember them. But the fact the resistance is present is an important symptom: where there is resistance, there unquestionably also is a repressed unconscious impulse striving to break through into consciousness; that indeed is the reason why the force of resistance is mobilized. *Compromise formations*—in this case, the manifest images of the dream—are meant to substitute for the repressed impulse in the only form the censorship will allow.

When, finally, resistance in its many and various expressions has been overcome, the free thoughts and images that run through one's consciousness, random and disconnected as they may seem, constitute the links of a chain along which it is possible to reach down to the repressed impulse—the latent content of the dream. This content will turn out to be a disguised wish fulfillment, in the majority of cases but not exclusively,[3] of an erotic and often infantile erotic character. Manifest dream images, thus, turn out to be substitute presentations—*symbols*—for the objects of that wish or, at any rate, to have some bearing on the repressed impulse.

The laws for the formation of the symbols that replace the objects of a repressed impulse are very complex. Their governing aim comes down to a matter of maintaining some, even if only remote, *connection* with the repressed presentation, on the one hand, and, on the other, of assuming a shape that would be wholly *legal*, correct, and acceptable for the conscious. This is accomplished by merging several images into one composite image, by interpolating a series of intermediary images linked both with the repressed presentation and with the one given in the manifest content of the dream, by implementing images of exactly opposite meaning, by transferring emotions and affects from their actual objects to other, indifferent details of the dream, by turning affects into their opposites, and the like.

Such is the technique for the formation of dream symbols.

What significance do these substitute images, these dream symbols, have? What purpose is served by these compromises between the conscious and the

---

[3] See *Handwörterbuch der Sexualwissenschaft*, p. 616.

unconscious, the permissible and the impermissible (but always wished for)? They serve as *safety valves* for repressed impulses and allow the unconscious to be *partially lived out*, thereby cleansing the psyche of energies held in and pent up in its depths.

The creation of symbols is partial compensation for the denial of satisfaction, under pressure from the reality principle, of all the organism's impulses and desires. It is a partial liberation, in compromise form, from reality, a return to the infantile paradise with its "all is permitted" and its hallucinatory wish fulfillment. The biological state of the organism during sleep is itself a partial resumption of the intrauterine situation of the foetus. We—unconsciously, of course—reenact that state, we play out a return to our mother's womb: We are undressed, we curl up under the blanket, we draw our knees up, bend our neck—in short, we recreate the foetal position; our organism is sealed away from all outside stimuli and influences; finally, our dreams, as we have seen, partially restore the reign of the pleasure principle.

Let us elucidate all that we have said with an illustration of a dream analysis produced by Freud himself.

The dream in question belongs to a man who had lost his father some years before. Freud begins by describing the manifest content of the dream:

> *His father was dead but had been exhumed and looked bad. He had been living since then and the dreamer was doing all he could to prevent him noticing it.* (The dream then went on to other and apparently very remote matters.)
>
> His father was dead; we know that. His having been exhumed did not correspond to reality; and there was no question of reality in anything that followed. But the dreamer reported that after he had come away from his father's funeral, one of his teeth began to ache. He wanted to treat the tooth according to the precept of Jewish doctrine: "If thy tooth offend thee, pluck it out." And he went off to the dentist. But the dentist said: "One doesn't pluck out a tooth. One must have patience with it. I'll put something into it to kill it; come back in three days and I'll take it out."
>
> "That 'take out'," said the dreamer suddenly, "that's the exhuming!"
>
> Was the dreamer right about this? It only fits more or less, not completely; for the *tooth* was not taken out, but only something in it that had died. But inaccuracies of this kind can, on the evidence of other experiences, well be attributed to the dream work. If so, the dreamer had condensed his dead father and the tooth that had been killed but retained; he had fused them into a unity. No wonder, then, that something senseless emerged in the manifest dream, for, after all, not everything that was said about the tooth could fit his father. Where could there possibly be a *tertium comparationis* between the tooth and his father, to make the condensation possible?
>
> But no doubt he must have been right, for he went on to say that he knew that if one dreams of a tooth falling out it means that one is going to lose a member of one's family.
>
> This popular interpretation, as we know, is incorrect or at least is correct only in a scurrilous sense. We shall be all the more surprised to find the topic thus touched upon reappearing behind other portions of the dream's content.

The dreamer now began, without any further encouragement, to talk about his father's illness and death as well as about his relations with him. His father was ill for a long time, and the nursing and treatment had cost him (the son) a lot of money. Yet it was never too much, he was never impatient, he never wished that after all it might soon come to an end. He was proud of his truly Jewish filial piety towards his father, of his strict obedience to Jewish law. And here we are struck by a contradiction in the thoughts belonging to the dream. He had identified the tooth and his father. He wanted to proceed with the tooth in accordance with Jewish law, which commanded him to pluck it out if it caused him pain or offence. He also wanted to proceed with his father, too, in accordance with the precepts of the law, but in this case it commanded him to spare no expense or trouble, to take every burden on himself, and to allow no hostile intention to emerge against the object that was causing him pain. Would not the two attitudes have agreed much more convincingly if he had really developed feelings toward his sick father similar to those toward his sick tooth—that is, if he had wished that an early death would put an end to his unnecessary, painful, and costly existence?

I do not doubt that this was really his attitude toward his father during the tedious illness and that his boastful assurances of his filial piety were meant to distract him from these memories. Under such conditions, the death wish against a father is apt to become active and to hide itself under the mask of such sympathetic reflections as that "it would be a happy release for him." But please observe that here we have passed a barrier in the latent dream thoughts themselves. No doubt the first portion of them was unconscious only temporarily—that is, during the construction of the dream; but his hostile impulses against his father must have been permanently unconscious. They may have originated from scenes in his childhood and have occasionally slipped into consciousness, timidly and disguised, during his father's illness. We can assert this with greater certainty of other latent thoughts which have made unmistakable contributions to the content of the dream. Nothing, indeed, is to be discovered in the dream of his hostile impulses towards his father. But if we look for the roots of such hostility to a father in childhood, we shall recall that fear of a father is set up because, in the very earliest years, he opposes a boy's sexual activities, just as he is bound to do once more from social motives after the age of puberty. This relation to his father applies to our dreamer as well: His love for him included a fair admixture of awe and anxiety, which had their source in his having been early deterred by threats from sexual activity.

The remaining phrases in the manifest dream can be explained now in relation to the masturbation complex. "*He looked bad*" is indeed an allusion to another remark of the dentist's to the effect that it looks bad if one has lost a tooth in that part of the mouth; but it relates at the same time to the "looking bad" by which a young man at puberty betrays, or is afraid he betrays, his excessive sexual activity. It was not without relief to his own feelings that in the manifest content the dreamer displaced the "looking bad" from himself on to his father—one of the kinds of reversal by the dream work which is familiar to you. "*He had been living since then*" coincides with the wish to bring back to life as well as with the dentist's promise that the tooth would survive. The sentence "the dreamer was doing all he could *to prevent him (his father) noticing it*" is very subtly devised to mislead us into thinking that it should be completed by the words "that he was dead." The only completion, however, that makes sense comes once more from the masturbation complex; in that connection it is self-evident that the young man did all he could to conceal his sexual life from his father. And finally, remember that we must always interpret what are called "dreams with a dental stimulus" as relating to masturbation and the dreaded punishment for it.

You can see how this incomprehensible dream came about. It was done by producing a strange and misleading condensation, by disregarding all the thoughts that were in the centre of the latent-thought-process and by creating ambiguous substitutes for the deepest and chronologically most remote of these thoughts.[4]

That is how a psychoanalytical interpretation of a dream works. The method of free association makes it possible, in the given case, to bring to light all the intermediary formations—the ailing tooth and the need to have it extracted—that connect the manifest images of the dream—*the father exhumed from his grave*—with a repressed unconscious impulse—*the infantile wish to be rid of one's father*. The latent thoughts of this dream—hostility toward the father and the urge to get rid of him—are so disguised in the manifest images that the dream fully satisfies the strictest moral requirements of consciousness. In all likelihood, Freud's patient did not find it easy to concur with the kind of interpretation Freud gave his dream.

This dream is interesting for the fact that its latent thoughts (secret wishes) provided outlet for hostility toward the patient's father that had been pent up in the patient's unconscious throughout his entire life. The dream condensed unconscious hostile impulses belonging to three periods of his life—the period of the Oedipus complex, the period of puberty (masturbation complex), and, finally, the period of the father's illness and death. In any case, the analytical probe plumbed to the very bottom of the dream—the infantile impulses of the Oedipus complex.

Freud uses the same methods for the analysis of other types of compromise formations, as well, particularly for investigation of the *pathological symptoms* of various nervous disorders. In point of fact, Freud came to dream interpretation out of concern with psychiatric needs and in the effort to utilize dreams as symptoms. Even though dream analyses were the material on which the method was elaborated, refined, and perfected, the prime material for drawing conclusions about the unconscious and its content was, of course, symptoms of nervous disorders.

We cannot delve into that interesting but highly specialized area here. We shall limit ourselves to a few brief remarks about the psychiatric application of this method of Freud's.

At a session of psychoanalytical treatment, the patient is supposed to tell the doctor everything that comes to mind concerning the symptoms and circumstances of his illness. The main aim in this case, as in dream interpretation, is to *overcome the resistance* that the patient's conscious brings to bear. But that

---

[4] *Standard Edition* 15 (1963): 188-190.

resistance at the same time serves as an important clue to the doctor: Wherever it flares up with particular force, there must be the patient's "sore point," which should become the doctor's main target of attention. We already know the dictum: *where there is resistance, there is repression*. The doctor's task is to dig down to the *repressed complexes* in the patient's psyche, because the root of all nervous disorders consists in the unsuccessful repression of some especially strong infantile complex (most often, the Oedipus complex). Once the complex is discovered, it must be given a chance to "drain," so to speak, into the patient's consciousness. In order for this to happen, the patient must "accept" the complex and then, with the doctor's help, thoroughly "live it out," that is, transform the *unsuccessful involuntary repression* (*Verdrängung*) of the complex into a *conscious and reasoned judgement* (*Verurteilung*) about it. In this way a cure is effected.

The psychoanalytical method was also applied by Freud to a host of very common *phenomena of everyday life*—slips of the tongue and pen, the forgetting of words and names, and so forth. Under analysis, all of these turned out to be compromise formations of the same type as dreams and pathological symptoms. To such phenomena Freud devoted a book called *The Psychopathology of Everyday Life*. Let us now consider a few examples from this area.

The president of the Austrian parliament once opened a parliamentary session with the words: "Gentlemen, I recognize that a quorum is present and, therefore, I declare the meeting closed."

He, of course, meant to say "open." What is the explanation for this slip of the tongue? The meeting promised to be a disagreeable one for him, and deep down he would have wished it were already over. And so this wish—a wish, needless to say, that he himself would never have acknowledged—infiltrated the statement he was making and, independently of his will and consciousness, produced a distortion.

Another example:

In his inaugural lecture, a certain professor intended to say: "I am not able (*Ich bin nicht geeignet*) to apprise all the merits of my esteemed predecessor." Instead he declared: "I am not apt (*Ich bin nicht beneigt*) to apprise, etc." Thus, instead of *"nicht geeignet"* (not able) he mistakenly used the similar sounding *"nicht geneigt"* (not apt). A quite different meaning came out than intended, but it in fact expressed the unconscious enmity that the professor felt toward his predecessor.[5]

Similar processes occur in cases of forgetting words and names. When we try to remember some appellation we have forgotten, other names and ideas arise in our consciousness that have some relationship to the forgotten item. These

---

[5] [Both examples are also found in *Introductory Lectures on Psycho-Analysis* (*Standard Edition* 15:4041). *Translator*.]

names and ideas that arise involuntarily are analogous to the *substitute images of dreams*. With their help we can work back to what we have forgotten. In such cases it always turns out that the *reason for the forgetting was some disagreeable remembrance associated in our mind with the forgotten appellation*. Exactly that was what had "allured into oblivion" the perfectly innocent word or name. Here is one such instance as reported by Freud:

> On one occasion a stranger had invited me to drink some Italian wine with him, but when we were in the inn it turned out that he had forgotten the name of the wine which he intended to order because of his very agreeable recollections of it. From a quantity of substitute ideas of different kinds which came into his head in place of the forgotten name, I was able to infer that thoughts about someone called Hedwig had made him forget the name. And he not only confirmed the fact that he had first tasted this wine when he was with someone of that name, but with the help of this discovery he recalled the name of the wine. He was happily married at the present time and this Hedwig belonged to earlier days which he had no wish to remember.[6]

Thus, the same psychical dynamics of conflict and compromise between the conscious and the unconscious, with which we are already familiar, extends, according to Freud, into the area of the most trivial phenomena of everyday life.

A further area of application for the psychoanalytical method is that of ideological formations in the strict and proper sense—myths, art, philosophical ideas, social and political phenomena. Of this area we shall speak in the next chapter.

[6] *Standard Edition* 15:111-112.

CHAPTER 6

Freudian Philosophy of Culture

*Culture and the unconscious. Myth and religion. Art. Forms of
social life. The trauma of birth.*

All ideological creativity, according to the Freudian doctrine, springs from
the same *psycho-organic* roots as do dreams and pathological symptoms; absolutely all aspects of creativity—in terms of repertoire as well as form and
content—can be traced back to these roots. Each factor in an ideological system
is strictly *determined along psychobiological lines*: It is a compromise product of
the struggle of forces within the organism, an index either of the equilibrium of
these forces or of the predominance of one. Just as with any pathological
symptom or obsession, an ideological construct draws its strength from the
depths of the unconscious. It differs from pathological phenomena in that it
involves *firmer and more steadfast* compromise agreements between the conscious and the unconscious, agreements that are equally advantageous to both
sides and, consequently, beneficial for the human psyche.[1]

In the Freudian philosophy of culture we meet all the "psychical mechanisms" already familiar to us, so that we need not take up too much time in our
examination of it.

The creation of *mythological images* is completely analogous to the "dream-
work." Myth is the collective dream of a community. The images in myths are
substitute symbols of repressed unconscious instincts. Of especially great importance are the myths connected with the experience and repression of the
Oedipus complex. The well-known Greek myth about Cronus devouring his
children, and his castration and murder at the hands of Zeus, who was saved by

[1] C. Jung, one of Freud's disciples, demonstrated a number of amazing coincidences
between the fantasies of a patient suffering from *Dementia praecox* and the myths of early
man. [*Editor's note*]

his mother's hiding him for a time within her body (return to the mother's womb), is one of the most typical examples of the kind. The derivation of all the symbols of this myth from the Oedipus complex is perfectly obvious. To the same set of myths belong legends about combat between father and son that are so widespread among all peoples: the combat of Hilderbrand and Hadubrand in the Germanic sagas, of Rustem and Zorab in the Persian, of Il'ja Muromec and his son in the Russian—these are all variations on one and the same perennial theme, *the struggle for possession of the mother*.

Religious systems are considerably more complex. Here, along with repressed complexes of sexual instincts, a major role is played by the unconscious superego. It is the Oedipus complex once again that supplies the nurturing ground for the development of religious ideas and cults. Depending on which of the two factors in the Oedipus complex attains predominance in religious experience—*the mother's power of attraction or the father's prohibitions and will*—religions are classified by Freudianism into matriarchal or patriarchal subdivisions. Typical examples of the former are the oriental religions of Astarte, Baal, and so on. The purest expression of a patriarchal religion is Judaism, with its prohibitions, commandments and, what is more, its rite of circumcision (symbol of the prohibition imposed by the father on the incestuous impulses of the son).

Let us now turn to art.

Freud himself applied his method of interpreting dreams and symptoms mainly to the aesthetic phenomena of *jokes and wit*.[2]

The forms of jokes are governed by the same laws that provide the formal structure of dream images, that is, the laws for the formation of substitute presentations with the same mechanism for bypassing the legal conscious through such devices as coalescence of words or images, substitution of images, verbal ambiguity, transference of meaning from one level to another, displacement of emotions, and so on.

Jokes and witticisms have the tendency to *bypass reality*, to provide relief from the *seriousness of life*, and to secure an outlet for repressed infantile impulses, whether sexual or aggressive.

Sexual jokes are the offspring of obscenity and are engendered as its aesthetic substitute. But what is obscenity? Obscenity is a *surrogate* for sexual performance, sexual satisfaction. Obscenity necessarily involves a women, that is, it is calculated on a woman's presence, whether real or imagined. Its intent is to induce a woman's sexual arousal. It is a technique of seduction. Saying the names of obscene objects is a surrogate for seeing them or displaying them or touching them. Decked out in the form of a joke, obscenity is better able to mask its true tendency, making it more acceptable for the cultural consciousness. A good joke

---

[2] Freud, *Der Witz und seiner Beziehung zum Unbewussten*, 3rd Edition (1921).

needs a listener; its aim is not only to bypass a prohibition but also to implicate the listener via laughter, to make the laughing listener an accomplice and, thereby, as it were, *socialize* the transgression.

In jokes of the aggressive sort, under cover of artistic form, free expression is given to *infantile hostility* toward any law, regulation, or national or social institution to which *the unconscious attitude toward the father and the father's authority* (*Oedipus complex*) or hostility toward any person not oneself (*infantile self-centeredness*) has been transferred.

Thus, a joke, too, is only a safety valve for pent-up energies in the unconscious; it, too, in the final analysis, serves the unconscious and is governed by it. The needs of the unconscious are what create the form and content of jokes.

No other works devoted specifically to the topic of art are found among Freud's own writings. It was Freud's students and disciples, especially Otto Rank, who pursued the study of this area further.

According to the Freudian writers on art, every artistic image always has reference to the unconscious but does so in a form that deceives and reassures the conscious. This deception is salutary: It enables certain common human complexes to be "lived out" without creating serious conflicts with the conscious.

Of particularly great importance for all forms of art are *erotic symbols*. Behind the most innocent-seeming and commonplace of artistic images some erotic object is always decipherable. An example from the field of Russian literature might be cited here. A certain Professor Ermakov of Moscow applied the psychoanalytical method to an interpretation of the famous story "Nose" by N. V. Gogol'. The nose in "Nose" turns out to be, according to Ermakov, a substitute symbol for the penis. Underlying the whole theme of the loss of one's nose and the particular motifs implementing that theme in the story is a complex closely associated with the Oedipus complex (in its father's threat aspect)—the *castration complex: fear of the loss of one's penis or one's sexual potency.*[3] Further examples we believe would be superfluous.

But it is not only from the unconscious "id" that art draws its powers; its source might also be the unconscious "superego." So, for instance, *unconscious feelings of guilt* (one of Dostoevskij's basic themes), the *imposition of severe ethical injunctions* (a basic motif of the later Tolstoj), and other related motifs emanating from the sphere of the superego can also feed into creative art, although, to be sure, such motifs find their greatest importance in philosophical constructs rather than art.

Thus, the entire content side of art derives from *premises in individual psychology*; it reflects the play of psychical forces in the individual human soul.

[3] I. D. Ermakov, *Očerki po psixologii gogolevskogo tvorčestva* [Essays in the Psychology of Gogol's Creative Art] (Moscow-Petrograd, 1923).

No room is left for the reflection of objective socioeconomic existence with its forces and conflicts. Wherever we do find images in art taken from the world of social and economic relations, we are to understand that these images, too, have significance only as substitutes—behind such images, as behind Major Kovalev's nose, invariably lurks somebody's erotic complex.

So far as the forms and techniques of art are concerned, psychoanalyists either pass over such issues in complete silence or they explain form in terms of the old principle of *the least expenditure of energy*. The formal in art is regarded as that which requires of the perceiver a minimal input of energy for a maximal result. This *principle of economy* (in a somewhat more sophisticated way, to be sure) was applied by Freud to the analysis of the technique of jokes and witticisms.

We must now briefly deal with the psychoanalytical theory of the *origin of social forms. Massenpsychologie und Ich-Analyse*, Freud's most recent book, is devoted to the fundamentals of this theory.

At the center of this whole psycho-sociological construct stand the already familiar identification mechanism and the superego.

We have seen that the superego (an aggregate of unconscious imperatives, calls to duty, conscience, and the like) is formed in the human psyche by way of identification *with the father* and other, *unpossessable* objects of a person's first love. The superego includes within its range of manifestations one important area of which we have not yet had occasion to speak. It is a common fact that a person in love, in most instances, is inclined to attribute to the object of his love all manner of virtues and perfections that the latter does not possess in reality. In such cases we say that a person is idealizing the object of his love. *The process of idealization is unconscious*; indeed, the lover himself is totally convinced that all these virtues do belong to the object and he does not so much as suspect the subjective nature of the process of idealization that is taking place within his own psyche. Furthermore, it is not only the object of sexual love, in the narrow sense, that can be idealized; we often also idealize our teachers, our superiors, our favorite writers and painters, exaggerating their good qualities and overlooking their faults. Moreover, we can even idealize an institution or an idea. In effect, the range of possibility for idealization is quite broad.

How does the psychical mechanism of idealization work? We might describe the idealization process as the reverse of the process of superego formation. In the latter case, we incorporate an object into ourselves, we enrich ourselves by its addition; in the former case, on the contrary, we *project into an object a part of ourselves, namely, our superego, and we enrich the object while impoverishing ourselves*. In cases of ordinary sexual infatuation this process rarely goes very far. But if we wholly expropriate our superego in the object's favor or, in other words, if we place the object in the superego's stead, we deprive ourselves of any possibility of counteracting the will and power of that object. Indeed, with what could we do so? It has taken the place of the superego—the place of our critical faculty and the place of our conscience! The will of such an authority is incontrovertible. It is in just such a manner that the power and authority of the leader, the priest, the state, the church are established.[4]

Thus, the voice of the father, which, internalized in the period of the Oedipus complex and become the inner voice of conscience, is now, by a reversed process, once again projected outward and becomes the voice of an external authority of an incontrovertible and sacrosanct character.

The very same process whereby one person's superego is replaced by the personality of another is what, according to Freud, underlies *hypnotic phenomena*, as well. The hypnotist appropriates the patient's superego and takes its place. From that position he easily controls the patient's weak conscious ego.

Needless to say, social organizations involve more than just this one-to-one relationship of an individual person to an authority figure—leader, priest, or other. Beside this relationship there is the fact of the *social solidarity* among all the members of a tribe, a church, a state. How is this fact to be explained? In Freud's view, it is to be explained by the same identification mechanism that we have already seen. Owing to the fact that all members of a tribe have transferred their superegos to one and the same object (the chief), they have no other course than to identify with one another and become equals, neutralizing their differences. That is how a tribe is formed.

Here is Freud's own summary definition: "A primary group . . . is a number of individuals who have substituted one and the same object for their ego ideal and have consequently identified themselves with one another in their egos."[5]

As the reader can see, Freud maintains that social organization is also wholly explainable in terms of psychical mechanisms. Psychical forces create human contacts, shape them, and give them solidity and durability. Meanwhile, conflicts with established social authority, social and political revolution, in most cases, have roots in the id—the id rebelling against the superego or, rather, rebelling against the external object standing in place of the superego. *The least significance in all areas of cultural creativity belongs to the conscious ego*. This ego adheres to the interests of reality (the external world) with which it attempts to reconcile the id's appetites and passions, while the superego, with its categorical demands, exerts its pressure on the ego from above. Thus, the conscious ego serves three mutually hostile masters—the external world, the id, and the superego—and endeavors to reconcile the conflicts that constantly arise among them. In cultural creativity the ego plays a *formal and constabulary role. The driving spirit, and the power and profundity, of culture are creations of the id and superego*.

[4] *Massenpsychologie und Ich-Analyse* (1921), Chapter 7.
[5] *Standard Edition* 18:116.

The tendencies inherent in the final stage of development of Freudianism have found their most extreme and acute expression, as already pointed out, in the book by Otto Rank called *The Trauma of Birth*. This book is something of a synthesis of Freudian philosophy of culture and to it we must turn in concluding our exposition of Freudianism.

It should be noted that Rank is Freud's favorite student and is considered the Freudian of greatest orthodoxy. His book is dedicated to his teacher and commemorates the latter's birthday. Under no circumstances can it be claimed as mere eccentricity. It expresses to the full the spirit of Freudianism today.

The entire life of a man and all his cultural creativity amount for Rank to nothing more or less than his *living out and overcoming, in various ways and with the help of various means, the trauma of birth*.

A man's birth into the world is traumatic: The organism, ejected from inside the mother's womb by the process of labor, experiences a terrible and excruciating shock the like of which will only come again with the shock of death. The horror and pain of the trauma are what initiated the human psyche; the trauma forms the bottom of the human soul. The terror of birth becomes the first experience to be repressed and the one onto which all subsequent repressions will be drawn from then on. The trauma of birth is the root of the unconscious and of the psychical in general. Throughout the rest of his life a man can never entirely be rid of the terror experienced at birth.

But together with this feeling of terror an urge to go back is engendered—an urge to return to the paradise experienced in the intrauterine state. This longing to return and this sense of horror constitute the basis for the ambivalent attitude that a person feels toward his mother's womb. It both attracts and repels. The "trauma of birth" determines the direction and meaning of personal life, and of cultural creativity, as well.

The *intrauterine state* is characterized by there being *no breach between need and its satisfaction*, that is, no breach between the *organism* and *its external reality*. Indeed, for the foetus there is no external world, properly speaking; its world is the mother's organism, which is a direct extension of its own organism. All the characteristic features of paradise and the Golden Age in myths and sagas, of the future world harmony of philosophical speculations and religious revelations and, finally, of the socioeconomic paradise of political utopias—all these clearly display unmistakable signs of their origin from that urge to return to the intrauterine life that all men once experienced. *All these notions have as their basis a vague, unconscious memory of a paradise that really did exist*, and that is why they exercise so powerful an effect on men's minds. They are not fictions, but their truth belongs not to the future but to every man's past. To be sure, the gates of paradise are guarded by a grim keeper—the terror of birth, which prevents that memory from being *fully awakened* and which causes the urge to return to the womb to be veiled in all manner of substitute images and symbols.

The trauma of birth appears in pathological symptoms: infantile phobias, adult neuroses and psychoses. It send shocks to the ill person's body, nonproductively repeating (in diminished form, to be sure) the actual shock experienced at the moment of birth. But the trauma is not lived out thereby. A genuine overcoming of this trauma is found only by way of cultural creativity. Rank defines culture as *the aggregate of efforts to transform the external world into a substitute, a surrogate (Ersatzbildung) of the mother's womb.*

All culture and industry are symbolic. We live in a world of symbols, all of which, in the final analysis, signify one thing—*the mother's womb* (more strictly, the uterus) and the accesses to it. What is the cave that primeval man sought refuge in? What is the room that we feel cosy in? What is homeland, state, etc.? They are all only surrogates for the mother's protective womb.

Rank has analyzed architectural forms and tries to prove their covert resemblance to the uterus. He derives the forms of art from the same source—the trauma of birth. So, for example, archaic statues that represent the human body in stooped or sitting postures unambiguously display the *foetal position*. Only the human being in Greek plastic art—the athlete at free play in the external world—signifies an overcoming of the trauma. The Greeks were the first to succeed in feeling at home in the external world; they were not drawn to the darkness and comfort of the intrauterine state. The Greeks had solved the riddle of the Sphinx, which was, according to Rank, none other than the riddle of human birth.

Thus, all creativity is conditioned, with respect to content as well as to form, by the act of birth into the world. However, by far the best surrogate of paradise, the fullest compensation for the trauma of birth, is, according to Rank, *sexual life. Coitus is a partial return to the womb.*

Death, Rank claims, is also preceived by man as a return to the womb. The fear associated with the thought of death repeats the terror of birth. The most ancient forms of burial—the hole dug in the ground ("Mother Earth"), the sitting position of the corpse with legs drawn up (foetal position), also burial in a boat (an allusion to the uterus and the amniotic fluid), the shape of the coffin, the rituals connected with burial—all these things reveal an unconscious conception of death as a return to the mother's womb. The Greek method of burning corpses again signifies the most successful overcoming of the trauma of birth. The final spasms of the death agony, as Rank sees it, exactly repeat the first spasms of the organism in the act of being born.

The methods Rank used in his work were completely subjective. He attempted no objective, physiological analysis of the trauma of birth and its possible effect on the subsequent life of the organism. He only sought to find reminiscences of the trauma in dreams, in pathological symptoms, in myths, art, and philosophy.

Highly characteristic of Rank's approach is his conception of the *psychoanalytical session* as a recapitulation of the act of birth (the very period of psychoanalytical treatment is normally about nine months): At the start, the patient's libido is focused on the doctor; the doctor's office is kept semi-dark (only the patient is located in the illuminated portion of it, the doctor sits in the half-light) and this represents the mother's womb for the patient. The end of treatment reproduces the trauma of birth: The patient is supposed to liberate himself from the doctor and, thereby, to work out his severance from his mother—all because the trauma of birth is the ultimate source of all nervous disorders.

With this we may conclude our exposition of Freudianism. Rank's book provides an excellent transition to the critical section of our study. It is a magnificent *reductio ad absurdum* of certain aspects of Freudianism.

PART III

A CRITICAL ANALYSIS
OF FREUDIANISM

CHAPTER 7

Freudianism as a Variant of Subjective Psychology

Freudianism and modern psychology. The elementary composition of the psyche and the unconscious. The subjectivism of the "dynamics" of the psyche. Critical analysis of the theory of erogenous zones. Freudianism and biology.

In our second chapter we characterized the two basic trends in modern psychology—the subjective and the objective. Now we must try to give an exact and detailed answer to the question regarding Freudianism's position with respect to those trends.[1]

Both Freud and his followers maintain that they have effected a radical reform of the old psychology and that through their efforts the foundation for an entirely new, objective science of psychology has been established.

Unfortunately, neither Freud nor any of his followers has ever made the slightest effort to elucidate precisely and concretely the Freudian position on contemporary psychology and its methods. The lack constitutes a major deficiency in Freudianism. The psychoanalytical school, after originally having been the target of unanimous persecution by the scientific community, withdrew into itself and adopted somewhat *sectarian modes* of operation and thought not altogether appropriate to scientific endeavors. It became the habit of Freud and his students to quote only themselves and refer only to one

---

[1] The critical literature on Freud is small. In addition to works already cited, let us mention Maag, "Geschlectsleben und seelische Störungen," in *Beiträge zur Kritik der Psychoanalyse* (1924); Otto Hinrichsen, *Sexualität und Dichtung* (1912); Edgar Michaelis, "Die Menschheits-Problematik der Freudschen Psychoanalyse," in *Urbild und Maske* (Leipzig, 1925).

another. In more recent times, they have begun quoting from Schopenhauer and Nietzsche, as well. The rest of the world hardly even exists for them.[2]

We repeat, Freud never made any serious attempt to delineate his doctrine with respect to other psychological trends and methods in concrete and detailed terms. Thus, we have no clear idea of his position with regard to the *introspective method*, the *laboratory-experimental method*, the *Wurtzburg school* (Messer and others,) *functional psychology* (Stumpf and others), *differential psychology* (W. Stern)[3] and more recent attempts at creating *objective methods* by the school of so-called American behaviorism. Nor was Freud's position ever made clear concerning the famous controversy over *psychophysical parallelism versus psychophysical causality* that so aroused the psychologists and philosophers of his generation.[4]

Whenever Freud and his students contrast their conception of the psychical to all other psychology—without, alas, even troubling themselves to differentiate that "other psychology"—they bring one accusation to bear against it: *its identification of the psychical with the conscious*. For psychoanalysis, in contrast, the conscious is but one of the psychical systems.

Is it, perhaps, that the difference between psychoanalysis and all other psychology is really so great that there can be nothing in common between them, not even that minimum of common language essential for comparison and delimitation? Freud and his students apparently are convinced that this is so.

But is it?

The fact of the matter is that *Freudianism transferred into its constructs all the fundamental defects of the subjective psychology of the time*. There is no difficulty ascertaining this fact, provided only we not let ourselves be misled by the sectarian but still, on the whole, impressive and apt terminology of the doctrine.

In the first place, Freudianism dogmatically appropriated the old categorization of mental phenomena—originating with J.-C. Tetens and made a philo-

---

[2] It must be said that official science up to the present time has still not fully legitimized Freudianism, while in academic circles it is even considered bad taste to talk about it. See, Wittels, *S. Freud, der Mann, die Schale, die Lehre* (1924). In Willie Moog's survey of German philosophy in the twentieth century (1923), Freud and psychoanalysis are not mentioned at all. In Müller-Freienfels's survey, there is only passing mention contained in a few lines.

[3] All of these were factions of subjective psychology contemporary with the first and second periods in the development of Freudianism.

[4] Freud himself does acknowledge psychophysical causality, but, at the same time, he displays the traits of a parallelist at every step of the way. Moreover, his entire method is based on the hidden, never articulated assumption that for everything somatic one could find corresponding psychical equivalents (in the unconscious psyche) and, consequently, it is possible to dispense with the somatic in and of itself and deal exclusively with its psychical counterparts.

sophical truism thanks to Kant—into Will (desires, drives), Feeling (emotions, affects) and Mind (sensations, presentations, thoughts). Moreover, it retains exactly the same definitions of these faculties as were in common use by the psychology of the time and, as we see, exactly the same differentiation among them. Indeed, if we take a look at the *elementary makeup* of the psyche, as Freudianism conceives of it, we find that it is composed of sensations, presentations, desires, and feelings, that is, of exactly those same elements out of which the old psychology had built the "mental life" of man. What is more, without the slightest critical qualification and, moreover, in their usual, then current meanings, all these psychical elements are transferred by Freud to the domain of the unconscious: In the unconscious, too, we find desires, feelings, presentations.

But these elements of psychical life, after all, exist only *for consciousness.* And the old psychology had produced its breakdown of the psyche into elementary components with the aid of the usual method of introspection, a method that, in its usual form, cannot take us beyond the confines of the "official conscious," as Freud himself asserts.

Introspection is indeed a thoroughly conscious process. Even the subjectivist psychologists, in the persons of some of their most eminent representatives, and a good deal before Freud, argued that introspection was not impartial (could not rid itself of value judgements), on the one hand, and, on the other, tended to *overrationalize* psychical life, and that, therefore, its evidence required substantial revision. In any case, introspection is possible only from a conscious point of view. The old psychology knew no other point of view and that is why it identified the psychical with the conscious.

Thus, it is clear that the breakdown of the psyche into the elements of feeling, will, and mind was dictated to the old psychology by none other than consciousness. The point of view of consciousness set the guidelines for laying down all the bases of subjective psychology.

But have we any right to construct the unconscious on analogy with the conscious and to assume that it contains exactly the same elements as we find in the conscious? Nothing gives us that right. Once consciousness is cast aside, it becomes totally senseless to retain feelings, presentations, and desires.

When a person self-consciously motivates his own actions, he can hardly help, of course, but refer to his feelings, desires, and presentations; but once we start analyzing those actions objectively, endeavoring to adhere consistently and throughout to the point of view of external apprehension, we shall find no such elements anywhere in the makeup of behavior. External, objective apprehension has to rely on different—*material*—elementary components of behavior, components that have nothing in common with desires, feelings, and presentations.

Thus, only in the light of subjective consciousness does the picture of our psychical life appear to us one of conflict of feelings, desires, and presentations.

Whatever real, objective forces might underlie that conflict, our self-consciousness can tell us nothing at all about it. If we attach the label "unconscious" to certain desires and feelings and the labels "preconscious" and "conscious" to others, we merely lapse into inner contradiction with ourselves but do not step out beyond the confines of subjective consciousness and the picture of psychical life open to it. Once the self-conscious point of view is cast aside, the whole of that picture and all of its component parts must also be rejected and a wholly different point of departure has to be sought for a conception of the psyche. That is exactly what objective psychology is doing. Freud, on the other hand, has tried erecting a completely new, quasi-objective edifice of the human psyche out of the old subjectivist bricks. What, after all, is "unconscious desire" if not the same old brick only turned around?

But Freudianism does even worse things than that. It not only transfers elements of the conscious to the unconscious, it *preserves fully intact in the unconscious the specific differences and logical distinctions of all these elements*. The unconscious turns out to be, if we follow Freud, a vivid and diverse world where all presentations and images correspond with perfect accuracy to specific referents, where all desires are specifically oriented and all feelings retain their entire wealth of nuances and delicate transitions.

Let us turn attention to the operation of the censorship. Freud considers the censorship a "mechanism" that operates completely *unconsciously* (the conscious, as the reader will recall, not only does not control the work of the censorship but does not even suspect its existence). Yet, how delicately this "unconscious mechanism" detects all the logical subtleties of thoughts and all the moral nuances of feelings! The censorship exhibits enormous ideological erudition and refinement; it makes purely logical, ethical, and aesthetic selections among experiences. Can this possibly be compatible with its unconscious, *mechanical* structure?

All of Freud's other "psychical mechanisms" display exactly the same supremely "conscious" and ideological character (for example, the transference mechanism that the reader now knows so well). Actually, the quality of a "mechanism" is what they have least of all. They belong not at all to the realm of physical nature; they are not naturalistic but *ideological*.

The concept of the unconscious, therefore, does not move the psyche the slightest bit closer to material nature; its implementation does not in the least help us connect a psychical system of laws with the objective system of laws for nature in general. The rift between the inner-subjective sphere and the material sphere remains exactly the same in psychoanalysis as in the psychology of consciousness.

Needless to say, all those methodological difficulties that inevitably accompany a breach in the integrity and consistency of external apprehension arise also in the case of Freudianism. Having taken a subjective position, psychoanalysis has deprived itself of a direct and unmediated approach to the material world.

It can have nothing to do with that world and must either ignore it altogether or dissolve it in the psychical world.

Freud and his students nowhere in fact deal *directly* with the material composition and material processes of the bodily organism; they look only for somatic reflections in the psyche, that is, in the final analysis, they also subordinate everything organic to the methods of introspection—they psychologize the organic.

Just such *psychologization of the somatic* is egregiously exhibited in Freud's doctrine on the erogenous zones. Freud makes no provision for a physiological theory of the erogenous zones, he takes no stock whatever of their chemistry or their physiological relationship with other parts of the body. It is only their psychical equivalents that he subjects to analysis and investigation, that is, he focuses attention on the role played by subjective presentations and desires, associated with the erogenous zones, in the psychical life of a human individual and from that individual's inner, introspective point of view.

The position and function in the total organization of the body of this or that erogenous zone (for example, the genitals)—the internal secretion of the sex glands, its influence on the operation and form of other organs, its relationship with the constitution of the body, and so on—all these processes, detectable in the external material world, are left completely undefined by Freud and in no real sense even taken into account.

How the role of an erogenous zone in the material composition of the body connects with the role it plays in the subjective psyche, taken in isolation, is a question for which Freud provides us no answer. As a result, we are presented with a kind of duplication of erogenous zones: *What happens with erogenous zones in the psyche becomes something completely separate and independent of what happens with them physically, chemically, and biologically in the material organism.*

These features of psychoanalysis take on particularly bold relief when Freud attempts to construct a theory of human character types on the basis of the erogenous zones doctrine. We shall mention here only one of the points in the theory that most acutely reveals its subjectivism.

Freud claims that the predominance of the anal zone in infantile eroticism leads to the development of specific character traits that will stay with a person throughout his life. Thus, the anal erotic develops the traits of frugality and parsimony and does so in the following way: The infant's fondness for holding back feces and prolonging the excretory act in order to achieve maximal pleasure from its performance is transformed in the adult (whose anal eroticism has been subjected to repression and has become unconscious) into a passion for holding onto and hoarding gold (money), which bears a resemblance to feces.

There is not a single word in this theory about any of the material bases of character formation that are inherent in the constitution of the body or about the physical or objective social effects of the environment. *The entire process of character formation runs its course within the confines of the subjective psyche viewed as an isolated entity*. Between holding back feces and holding onto money, between feces and gold, there is only the most farfetched, subjective resemblance, but there are no real, no material connections that might bind them together in the material composition of the organism itself or in the environment, that is, there is nothing to support that resemblance in objective apprehension. Thus, in Freud's way of looking at it, the erogenous zones determine a person's character and behavior (for, after all, a person's character is wholly inseparable from its expression in his behavior) *in complete disassociation from the body, the bodily constitution, and, in general, from any kind of material environment*.

That Freud should take such an attitude toward the material composition of the organism is wholly understandable. Inner experience, extracted by means of introspection, cannot in fact be directly linked with the data of objective, external apprehension. To maintain a thorough consistency only the one or the other point of view can be pursued. Freud has ultimately favored the consistent pursuit of the inner, subjective point of view; all external reality is for him, in the final analysis, merely the "reality principle," a principle that he places *on the same level* with the "pleasure principle."

Certain Freudians (Rank, Pfister, Groddeck) claim that psychoanalysis has succeeded in detecting a wholly unique realm of being, a realm neither of physical being nor of psychical being but of *neutral* being, as it were, out of which, by way of differentiation, both physical and psychical being can subsequently emerge.

It is to this kind of neutral being that the deepest levels of the unconcious belong; only at its very highest levels—those closest to the preconscious—does differentiation between mind and body begin to take place.

Such an assertion on the part of the Freudians mentioned is, of course, philosophically naive in the extreme. It completely bypasses the *question of method*, a question, in this instance, of decisive importance.

We might ask: In the purview of which kind of apprehension—internal or external—is this neutral being present and does its process of differentiation occur?

The Freudians mentioned studiously avoid this question. But we know that we shall find no being of this sort in the purview of external apprehension. There we find *a process of the extreme complication of organized matter* that leads, at some specific point, to the manifestation of the psyche as a *new quality of that matter*. But of course nowhere in the purview of external apprehension do we ever find the issuance of matter and psyche from some third thing. We have to do here with a naive metaphysical assertion that draws its material from internal, subjective apprehension but decks it out in a fictitious neutral form.

Certain partisans of Freud claim, having primarily his "theory of instincts" in mind, that psychoanalysis has its objective basis in biology.

This claim is completely groundless. One can with greater right speak of Freud's psychologization and subjectivization of biology. Freud dissolves all objective biological forms and organismic processes in the subjective-psychical. All those biological terms, with which the pages of psychoanalytical books teem, lose their objective rigor, so thoroughly dissolved are they in the subjective-psychological context.

To substantiate this point we need only cite Freud's classification of instincts.

All instincts other than the sexual are lumped together by Freud into the one set of *ego instincts*—the *Ich-triebe*. The flagrantly subjectivist principle of this classification is perfectly clear. It hardly need be said that such a classification is inadmissible from the rigorous biological point of view. Even the vitalists, extreme as they are, have never openly acknowledged a belief that biology could have anything to do with "I."

As for Freud's second, revised classification of instincts (that of the third period), it has taken on an overtly metaphysical character. Eros, stripped of any specific somatic source and extended to cover all manifestations of organic life without exception, is in no way superior to Bergson's "élan vital" or Schopenhauer's "Will"; and the death instinct is in no way superior to gravitation toward Nirvana.

Thus, *psychoanalysis in every respect faithfully adheres to the point of view of internal, subjective apprehension*. Viewed in terms of fundamental methodology, it does not differ in any essential way from the psychology of consciousness. It is another species of subjective psychology and nothing more. In the final analysis, psychoanalysis, too, relies on the data of introspection. To be sure, it gives these data a different interpretation—it attempts to build them into a different picture of the human psyche. But no matter how you interpret subjective data, if you remain on the grounds of internal apprehension, you will still get nothing objective out of them. In order to do so, you must change the point of view itself. That precisely is what Freud has not done.

CHAPTER 8

The Dynamics of the Psyche as a Struggle of Ideological Motives and Not of Natural Forces

The novelty of Freudianism. The dynamics of the psyche as a struggle of motives. The projection of social dynamics into the individual. The projection of the conscious present into the unconscious part. Facts and constructs. The objective factors of the dynamics of the psyche.

We have now ascertained that Freudianism is merely one species of subjective psychology. We have also seen wherein consists the common ground upon which Freudianism and all other subjectivist doctrines converge. But the issue is not exhausted thereby; we must also make a clear-cut delimitation and proper assessment of what it is precisely that *distinguishes Freudianism* from other subjectivist trends.

For, indeed, there is something paradoxically novel and original about Freudianism that strikes every newcomer to the doctrine. This impression of novelty most likely also formed in our reader's mind as he followed our exposition of psychoanalysis. This is something we must look into.

What immediately strikes one upon first acquaintance with Freud's doctrine and what remains the final and strongest impression of the entire construction is, of course, the *strife*, the *chaos*, the *adversity* of our psychical life, that run conspicuously throughout Freud's whole conception and that he himself referred to as the "dynamics" of the psyche.

In this respect Freudianism is really quite different than all other psychological trends. Mental life for the old psychology was all "peace and quiet": everything put right, everything in its place, no crises, no catastrophes; from birth to death a smooth, straight path of steady and purposive progress, of gradual mental growth, with the adult's consciousness of mind coming to replace the child's innocence. This naive *psychological optimism* is a characteristic feature of all pre-Freudian psychology. The only difference was that in some cases this optimism was expressed explicitly, while in others it permeated the whole picture of human mental life in more covert form.

This psychological optimism was the legacy of the *biological optimism* that reigned in science before Darwin. It amounted to the naive notion of the omniscient purposiveness of the living organism, a notion finally replaced by the Darwinian doctrine on the struggle for existence, the extinction of the weak, and the survival and propagation of only the fittest minority. A strict concept of natural necessity came to prevail in all domains of post-Darwinian biology. Only the psyche, governed by perspicacious consciousness, remained as the last refuge for the concepts of purposiveness, harmony, and so on, that had been expelled from all other fields. The psychical stood as the realm of harmony and order in opposition to the natural and the elemental.

To all appearances, Freudianism did produce a most radical change in these views on the psyche.

The human psyche belongs to the realm of nature, human psychical life is part of elemental life—that above all was the message the public at large seized upon out of the entire doctrine of Freud. Those people inclined toward Nietzscheanism (and there were quite a few of them among Freud's admirers) preferred to speak rather of the "tragicness of psychical life."

Apropos the last point, it should immediately be noted that while natural necessity is certainly a stranger to purposiveness and harmony, it is no less remote from tragedy. However, perhaps that expression ought not be taken as characterizing Freudianism as a whole.

Now, did Freud really succeed in detecting Nature in our psyche? Are the conflicts of the "ego," "id," and "superego," the "death instinct" and "Eros" really the conflicts of elemental forces? Or are they perhaps only conflicts of motives in the individual human consciousness? If that is the case, then we have something more like a "storm in a teacup" than a conflict of elemental forces.

In order to answer this question, it behooves us to restate in a somewhat different connection a set of ideas that we began to develop in the preceding chapter.

Freud's whole psychological construct is based fundamentally on human verbal utterances; it is nothing but a special kind of interpretation of utterances. All these utterances are, of course, constructed in the *conscious sphere of the psyche*. To be sure, Freud distrusts the surface motives of consciousness; he tries instead to penetrate to deeper levels of the psychical realm. Nevertheless, Freud does not take utterances in their objective aspect, does not seek out their physiological or social roots; instead he attempts to find the true motives of behavior in the utterances themselves—the patient is himself supposed to provide him information about the depths of the "unconscious."

Thus, Freud's construct remains within the confines of what a person himself can say about himself and his behavior on the basis of his own internal apprehension. Freud, to be sure, directs introspection along new pathways, makes it penetrate other levels of the psyche, but *he does not relinquish introspection as the sole method of authenticating the reality of psychical events*. The "unconscious," too, can and should be included in the sphere of introspection. After all, the patient is himself supposed to recognize the content of the "unconscious" (some repressed complex, for instance), to recall it, to attest to its existence with the aid of introspection. It is only in this way that a repressed "unconscious" experience acquires the value of a psychological fact.

For introspection, all the products of the unconscious take the forms of desires or impulses, find *verbal* expression and in *that* shape, that is, in the shape of a *motive*, enter into a person's awareness.

It is completely understandable that, in Freud's doctrine, the interrelations prevailing between the conscious and the unconscious should be so thoroughly unlike the relations between two *material* forces that allow of a precise objective account. Indeed, Freud's "conscious" and "unconscious" are ever at odds; between them prevail mutual hostility and incomprehension and the endeavor to deceive one another. Surely interrelations of this sort are only possible between two ideas, two ideological trends, two antagonistic persons, and not between two natural, material forces! Is it conceivable, for instance, that two natural forces engage in mutual deception or mutual nonrecognition?

Of course, only after entering into consciousness and donning the forms of consciousness (the forms of desires, thoughts, etc. with specific content) can products of the unconscious engage in conflict with ethical precepts or be perceived as deception of the "censorship."

Thus, *the whole of Freud's psychical "dynamics" is given in the ideological illumination of consciousness*. Consequently, *it is not a dynamics of psychical forces but only a dynamics of various motives of consciousness*.

In the whole Freudian construct of a psychical conflict, together with all the mechanisms through which it operates, we hear only the biased voice of the subjective consciousness interpreting human behavior. The unconscious is nothing but one of the motives of that consciousness, one of its devices for interpreting behavior ideologically.

What is the consciousness of an individual human being if not the ideology of his behavior? In this respect we may certainly compare it with ideology in the strict sense—as the expression of class consciousness. But no ideology, whether of person or class, can be taken at its face value or at its word. An ideology will lead astray anyone who is incapable of penetrating beyond it into the hidden play of objective material forces that underlies it.

For instance, a religious creed deludes only a person who believes in it and naively takes it for what it claims itself to be. But for the Marxist historian this same creed may present an extremely important and valuable document faith-fully reflecting certain social contradictions and interests of specific groups of people. He can bring to light the real economic and social conditions that inevitably gave rise to the religious creed in question.

That is how the objectivist psychologist works: He does not take verbal utterances on trust—or any motivation or explanation that a person himself, on the basis of his own inner apprehension, might give his behavior. He tries to discover the objective roots not only of a person's behavior as a whole but of his verbal utterances, as well. No longer will these utterances be able to lead him astray. They will be for him an accurate expression of objective conditions of behavior—physiological and socioeconomic conditions. Behind the "dynamics" of the psyche, behind the conflict of motives, the objectivist psychologist reveals the material dialectics of nature and history.

That is not how Freud works. Freud lets himself be drawn into the conflict of subjective motivations of consciousness. The fact that he prefers a special set of motives—unconscious ones—and extracts such motives in a special way does not change matters in the least. A motive remains a motive—it does not acquire the weight of a material phenomenon. Freud's system provides us no access to the fertile grounds of objective apprehension.

But where do all those "forces" with which Freud populates the psyche come from—the "ego," "the id," the "superego" and so forth?

The conflict of motives supplies no evidential grounds for these forces. The conflict of motives is a real phenomenon accessible to objective apprehension—after all, it finds expression in verbal utterances. Psychical forces, on the contrary, are arbitrary constructs that Freud utilizes in the effort to explain that conflict. As is true of the majority of constructs in subjective psychology, Freud's theory is a "projection" of certain objective relations of the external world into the world of the psyche. What finds expression there is, in the very first instance, the extremely complex *social interrelationship between doctor and patient*.

In what does this interrelationship consist?

A patient wishes to hide from the doctor certain of his experiences and certain events of his life. He wants to foist on the doctor his own point of view on the reasons for his illness and the nature of his experiences. The doctor, for his part, aims at enforcing his authority as a doctor, endeavors to wrest confessions from the patient and to compel him to take the "correct" point of view on his illness and its symptoms. Intertwining with all this are other factors: Between doctor and patient there may be differences in sex, in age, in social standing, and, moreover, there is the difference of their professions. All these factors complicate their relationship and the struggle between them.

And it is in the midst of this complex and very special social atmosphere that the verbal utterances are made—the patient's narratives and his statements in conversation with the doctor—utterances that Freud places squarely at the basis of his theory. Can we acknowledge these utterances as the expression of the patient's individual psyche?

Not a single instance of verbal utterance can be reckoned exclusively to its utterer's account. Every utterance is *the product of the interaction between speakers* and the product of the broader context of the whole complex *social situation* in which the utterance emerges. Elsewhere[1] we have attempted to show that any product of the activity of human discourse—from the simplest utterance in everyday life to elaborate works of literary art—derives shape and meaning in all its most essential aspects not from the subjective experiences of the speaker but from the social situation in which the utterance appears. Language and its forms are the products of prolonged social intercourse among members of a given speech community. An utterance finds language basically already prepared for use. It is the material for the utterance and it sets constraints on the utterance's possibilities. What is characteristic for a given utterance specifically—its selection of particular words, its particular kind of sentence structure, its particular kind of intonation—all this is the expression of the interrelationship between the speakers and of the whole complex set of social circumstances under which the exchange of words takes place. Those "psychical experiences" of the speaker, the expression of which we are inclined to see in his utterance, are, however, only in fact a one-sided, simplified, and scientifically unverifiable interpretation of a more complex social phenomenon. What we have here is a special kind of "projection," a means whereby we project into the "individual soul" a complex set of social interrelationships. Discourse is like a "scenario" of the immediate act of communication in the process of which it is engendered, and this act of communication is, in turn, a factor of the wider field of communication of the community to which the speaker belongs. In order to understand this "scenario," it is essential to reconstruct all those complex social interrelations of which the given utterance is the ideological refraction.

Nothing changes at all if, instead of outward speech, we are dealing with inner speech. Inner speech, too, assumes a listener and is oriented in its construction toward that listener. Inner speech is the same kind of product and expression of social intercourse as is outward speech.

All those verbal utterances of the patient (his verbal reactions), on which Freud's psychological system depends, are also just such *scenarios*, scenarios, first and foremost of the immediate, small social event in which they were engendered—the *psychoanalytical session*. Therein that complex struggle between doctor and patient, of which we spoke above, finds expression. What is reflected in these utterances is not the dynamics of the individual psyche but the *social dynamics* of the interrelations between doctor and patient. Here is the

---

[1] See our article, "Slovo v žizni i slovo v poèzii" [Discourse in Life and Discourse in Art], *Zvezda* 6 (1926). [An English translation of this article appears on pp. 93–116 of this book. *Translator*]

source for the dramatism that marks the Freudian construct. It is also the source for that personification of psychical forces which we have already mentioned. Here, indeed, people, not natural forces, are in conflict.

The psychical "mechanisms" readily disclose their social derivation to us. The "unconscious" stands in opposition not to the individual conscious of the patient but, primarily, to the doctor, his requirements and his views. "Resistance" is likewise primarily resistance to the doctor, to the listener, to the *other* person generally.

Freud's system *projects* the entire dynamics of the interrelationship between two people into the individual psyche. This sort of projection comes as no surprise; it is, as we have already said, a common phenomenon in subjective psychology. Psychical experiences, in the majority of instances, merely duplicate the world of external objects and social relations. Subjective idealism was only being consistent when it asserted that the whole world is nothing but the experience of the subject. When contemporary psychology attempts to draw a borderline between experience and things, it is compelled ultimately to come to the paradoxical conclusion that there is so such borderline, that everything depends on the point of view. One and the same thing, depending on the connection and the context in which we perceive it, is now a psychical experience (my sensation, my presentation), now a physical body or social phenomenon. The most radical conclusions in this regard were reached by one of the most eminent representatives of subjective psychology, William James. In his famous article "Does 'Consciousness' Exist?" James comes to the conclusion that *things and thoughts are made of the same material, that consciousness does not introduce a new reality into the world*—it is only *another point of view* on those very same things and phenomena.

Thus, Freudian psychical dynamics and its mechanisms are only a projection into the individual psyche of social interrelationships. It makes for a complex, dramatically charged image, and Freud employs it in his effort to interpret various aspects of human behavior, remaining within the confines of only one sector of that behavior—*the verbal reactions of human beings*.

We must turn attention to still another aspect of the Freudian system. The content of the unconscious, that is, various repressed complexes (including above all the Oedipus complex), is relegated by Freud to a person's past, to his early years of childhood. But the entire doctrine on these early, preconscious stages of human development is built on the basis of evidence supplied by adults. Those few attempts the Freudians did make to analyze the behavior of children *directly*[2] did not have, and could not have had, any substantive importance for

---

[2] The most important work of Freud's devoted to analysis of childhood nervous disorders is: "Geschichte der Fobie eines 5-jährigen Knaben," in *Kleine Schriften zur Neurosenlehre*, Part 3.

the working out of the Freudian construct. That construct took shape independently of such attempts and even before they were made, and the analyses themselves already presupposed and entirely depended on it. Thus, the whole construct of infantile complexes was obtained by *retrospective means*; it is based on the interpretation of the remembrances of adults and of those compromise formations with the aid of which those remembrances could be reached (let us recall here the dream analysis quoted above that delved down to the hidden remembrances of the Oedipus complex).

Can such a retrospective method of reconstructing experiences from early childhood (a complex, after all, is a set of experiences)—can such a method be considered scientifically sound?

We believe that nothing real, nothing objective can possibly be arrived at that way. What we are dealing with here is, in fact, a very widespread and typical phenomenon: *the interpretation of the past from the point of view of the present.* Anything like objective remembrance of our past inner experiences is, of course, entirely out of the question. We see in the past only what is important for the present, important for the instant in which we remember our past. We transfer from the present to the preconscious past of the child above all that ideological-evaluative complexion which is characteristic of the present only. All those evaluations, points of view, associations that have coalesced in the conscious period of our life with such concepts as "love," "sexual attraction," "mother," endowing these concepts with their own complexion and making them meaningful for us, are what we then transfer to the interpretation of the facts of childhood and thereby create out of these facts of childhood coherent and meaningful events like those of adult life.

"Sexual attraction to the mother," "the father rival," "hostility toward the father," "wish for the father's death"—if we subtract from all these "events" that ideational significance, that evaluative tone, that full measure of ideological weight which accrue to them only in the context of our conscious "adult" present, what would they have left?

They would, in any case, retain nothing that would give us the serious right to speak about an Oedipus complex, that is, about a repetition of the scheme of the Oedipus tragedy in a child's life. Precisely that aspect which gives the tragedy its profound and harrowing meaning, which horrifies and astounds the audience— that aspect would certainly be missing.

What would remain, then? A number of piecemeal objective observations that can be made about the behavior of a child: the early excitability of the sexual organs (e.g., infant erection) and of other erogenous zones, the difficulty of weaning a child away from his constant closeness to his mother's body (particularly, of course, the breast), and so on. There is obviously no need to contest a set of facts of this sort—they are commonly accepted facts. But from a series of such facts to the grandiose and startling construct of the Oedipus complex there is a vast abyss. Once you give up projecting into the past the points of view, evaluations, and interpretations that belong to the present, then you have no cause to speak about any such thing as an Oedipus complex, no matter how great the quantity of objective facts cited in proof.

The Freudians often challenge their critics by saying: If you want to refute the psychoanalytical theory, then you must first refute the facts on which it rests.

That sort of statement is already wrong in its assumptions. It distorts the actual state of affairs. Freudianism is not at all a series of facts and not at all that minimum of a working hypothesis necessary for preliminary organization and classification of those facts. Freudianism is a grandiose construct based on an extremely daring and original interpretation of facts, a construct that would not cease to astound us as something strange and paradoxical even if all the external facts advanced to prove it were accepted.

Facts are tested and verified or rejected by repeated observations or control experiments. But they can have no reflection on one's critical attitude toward the bases of the theoretical construct. Let us take Rank's thoroughly outlandish construct, the "trauma of birth." In order to declare this theory, at the very least, improbable, do we really need to refute the fact that the organism experiences a physiological shock at the moment the child is born into the world (the action of expulsion, the spasm of the first breath of air into the lungs, the effect of the atmosphere and so on)? The fact itself is correct (although it has still not been subjected to detailed scientific investigation) and is a piece of common knowledge. And all the same, when you read Rank's book you cannot help but wonder: Does he mean all this "seriously" or is he doing it "on purpose"?

Exactly the same thing has to be said about the relation of the facts of infantile sexuality to the construct of the Oedipus complex. The facts cannot confirm the Oedipus complex because the facts belong to a different level, a different set of dimensions, than it does. The facts pertain to external, objective apprehension; the construct, to the sphere of inner experiences in a child's psyche. Moreover, in order to have any right at all to speak of infantile sexuality, the word "sexuality" has to be understood to mean only a set of strictly defined physiological manifestations. If, on the contrary, we have in mind experiences pertaining to internal apprehension, experiences that are associated with those physiological manifestations but are permeated with value judgements and points of view, then we are making an arbitrary construct; instead of the physiological fact of sexuality, we take its ideological formulation. *The construct of the Oedipus complex is just such a purely ideological formulation projected into the psyche of a child*. The Oedipus complex is not at all the unadulterated expression of objective physiological facts.

The same must also be said about the other factors in the content of the unconscious. Everything involved here is a projection into the past of ideological interpretations of behavior that are characteristic for the present only. Freud nowhere steps beyond the confines of a subjective construct.

What, then, remains of the "dynamics" of the psyche once we subtract the constructs that are untenable for us?—Conflicts within the verbalized behavior of human beings. A struggle of motives, but not a struggle of natural forces.

Behind this struggle, as behind any ideological struggle of whatever scale, certain objective, material processes are covertly present. But Freudianism has not disclosed these processes. Indeed, to discover them would require going beyond the limits of subjective psychology, going beyond the limits of everything that a person himself could say about himself on the basis of his own inner apprehension, no matter how broadly that apprehension be understood.

Certain of these objective facts of behavior are physiological (ultimately, physiochemical) in character. Such facts can be studied by the methods that form the basis of the reflex doctrine of Academician Pavlov and his school or by the methods that have been so brilliantly and soundly argued by the late Jacques Loeb in his renowned theory of tropisms[3] or by other variants of the basically unitary physiological method. But when it comes to an explanation of human behavior all this supplies us very little. In particular, those conflicts of verbalized behavior, with which Freudianism confronts us, need, if they are to be properly understood, a rigorous and thoroughgoing account of socioeconomic factors. Only with the help of the flexible methods of dialectical materialism have we the possibility of illuminating those conflicts.

What we call the "human psyche" and "consciousness" reflects the dialectics of history to a much greater degree than the dialectics of nature. The nature that is present in them is nature already in economic and social refraction.

The content of the human psyche—a content consisting of thoughts, feelings, desires—is given in a formulation made by consciousness and, consequently, in the formulation of human verbal discourse. Verbal discourse, not in its narrow linguistic sense, but in its broad and concrete sociological sense—*that* is the *objective milieu* in which the content of the psyche is presented. It is here that motives of behavior, arguments, goals, evaluations are composed and given external expression. It is here, too, that arise the conflicts among them.

It is not within the purposes of a critique such as ours to introduce a positive program on the motives and conflicts of verbalized behavior. We can only point out the direction in which an objective understanding and study of these phenomena could be made possible.

---

[3] See Jacques Loeb, *Forced Movements, Tropisms, and Animal Conduct* (Philadelphia and London, 1918) and [original English title unknown. *Translator*] "Značenie tropizmov dlja psixologii" [The Significance of Tropisms for Psychology], *Novye idei v filosofii*, No. 8.

CHAPTER 9

The Content of Consciousness
as Ideology

*The sociological character of verbal reactions. Methods for
studying the content of consciousness. The concept of "behavioral ideology." The various levels of "behavioral ideology."
The sexual. Conclusions.*

We know that Freudianism began from a position of distrust of the conscious
and fundamental criticism of motives such as those a person is likely, in all
honesty and sincerity, to use as explanations for and commentary on his
behavior (let us recall Bernheim's experiment). Consciousness is in fact *that
commentary* which every adult human being brings to bear on every instance of
his behavior. According to Freud, this commentary is invalid; any psychology
that takes such commentary as its basis is likewise invalid.

Wherever Freud criticizes the psychology of consciousness, we can join in full
accord with him: A person's conscious motivation of his actions is certainly in
no instance to be taken as a scientific explanation of his behavior. But we go
further than that: Neither do the motives of the unconscious explain his
behavior in the least, for, as we have seen, the Freudian unconscious does not
fundamentally differ from consciousness; it is only another form of consciousness, only an ideologically different expression of it.

The motives of the unconscious that are disclosed at psychoanalytical sessions with the aid of "free association" are just such *verbal reactions* on the
patient's part as are all other, ordinary motives of consciousness. They differ
from the latter not in kind of "being," that is, ontologically, but only in terms
of content, that is, *ideologically,* In this sense Freud's unconscious can be called
the "unofficial conscious" in distinction from the ordinary "official conscious."

From the objective point of view, both sets of motives, those of the
unofficial as well as of the official conscious, are given completely alike in inner

and in outward speech and both alike are not a cause of behavior but a component, an integral part of it. For objective psychology, every human motive belongs to human behavior as a part of it and not a cause of it. Human behavior may be said to break down into motor reactions ("acts" in the narrow sense of the word) and reactions of *inner and outward speech* (verbal reactions) that accompany motor reactions. Both these components of the whole of human behavior are objective and material in nature and require for their explanation factors that are likewise objective and material with respect both to the human organism itself and to the surrounding natural and social environment.

The verbal component of behavior is determined in all the fundamentals and essentials of its content by objective-social factors.

The social environment is what has given a person words and what has joined words with specific meanings and value judgements; the same environment continues ceaselessly to determine and control a person's verbal reactions throughout his entire life.

Therefore, nothing verbal in human behavior (inner and outward speech equally) can under any circumstances be reckoned to the account of the individual subject in isolation; the verbal is not his property but the property of his *social group* (his social milieu).

In the preceding chapter we pointed out that every concrete utterance always reflects the *immediate* small social event—the event of communication, of exchange of words between persons—out of which it directly arose. We saw that Freud's "dynamics" reflected the psychoanalytical session with its struggle and peripeteia—that social event out of which the patient's verbal utterances were engendered. In the present chapter what interests us is not the immediate context of utterance but the broader, more enduring and steadfast social connections out of whose dynamics are generated all elements of the form and content of our inner and outward speech, the whole repertoire of value judgements, points of view, approaches, and so on with the help of which we illuminate for ourselves and for others our actions, desires, feelings, and sensations.

This content of our consciousness and of our psyche in its entirety and, likewise, the separate and individual utterances with the help of which that content and that psyche manifest themselves outwardly are in every respect determined by socioeconomic factors.

We shall never reach the real, substantive roots of any given single utterance if we look for them within the confines of the single, individual organism, even when that utterance concerns what appears to be the most private and most intimate side of a person's life. Any motivation of one's behavior, any instance of self-awareness (for self-awareness is always verbal, always a matter of finding some specifically suitable verbal complex) is an act of gauging oneself against some social norm, social evaluation—is, so to speak, the socialization of oneself and one's behavior. In becoming aware of myself, I attempt to look at myself, as it were, through the eyes of another person, another representative of my social group, my class. Thus, *self-consciousness*, in the final analysis, always leads us to *class consciousness*, the reflection and specification of which it is in all its fundamental and essential respects. Here we have the *objective roots* of even the most personal and intimate reactions.

How do we reach those roots?

With the help of those objective-sociological methods that Marxism has worked out for the analysis of various ideological systems—law, morality, science, world outlook, art, religion.

In bourgeois philosophy the contention has long held sway, and is even now quite widespread, that a work of cultural creativity can be considered fully explained if the analyst succeeds in reducing it to the specific individual states of mind and psychical experiences of the person who created it. This contention, as we have seen, is upheld by the Freudians, as well. But in actual fact there is no fundamental dividing line between the content of the individual psyche and formulated ideology. In any case, the content of the individual psyche is not the least bit easier to understand or clearer than the content of cultural creativity and, therefore, cannot serve as explication for it. An experience of which an individual is conscious is already ideological and, therefore, from a scientific point of view, can in no way be a primary and irreducible datum; rather, it is an entity that has already undergone ideological processing of some specific kind. The haziest content of consciousness of the primitive savage and the most sophisticated cultural monument are only extreme links in the single chain of ideological creativity. Between them exists a whole unbroken series of degrees and transitions.

The more clarified a thought of mine becomes, the closer it will approach the formulated products of scientific creativity. What is more, my thought will be able to achieve final clarity only when I find exact verbal formulation for it and bring it into contact with scientific postulations that have a bearing on the same topic—in other words, my thought will not achieve final clarity until I transform it into an authoritative scientific product. Similarly, a feeling cannot achieve culmination and definitiveness without finding its external expression, without nurturing itself on words, rhythm, color, that is, without being forged into a work of art.

The route leading from the content of the individual psyche to the content of culture is a long and hard one, but it is a single route, and throughout its entire extent at every stage it is determined by one and the same socioeconomic governance.

At all stages of this route the human consciousness operates through words—that medium which is the most sensitive and at the same time the most complicated refraction of the socioeconomic governance. For the study of verbal reactions in their most primitive, pragmatic form, the same methods must be used as Marxism has worked out for the study of complex ideological constructs, since the laws of the refraction of objective necessity in verbal discourse are one and the same in both instances.

Any human verbal utterance is an ideological construct in the small. The motivation of one's behavior is juridical and moral creativity on a small scale; an exclamation of joy or grief is a primitive lyric composition; pragmatic considerations of the causes and consequences of happenings are germinal forms of scientific and philosophical cognition, and so on and so forth. The stable, formulated ideological systems of the sciences, the arts, jurisprudence, and the like have sprung and crystallized from that seething ideological element whose broad waves of inner and outward speech engulf our every act and our every perception. Of course, an ideology, once it has achieved formulation, exerts, in turn, a reverse influence on our verbal reactions.

Let us call that inner and outward speech that permeates our behavior in all its aspects "behavioral ideology." This behavioral ideology is in certain respects more sensitive, more responsive, more excitable and livelier than an ideology that has undergone formulation and become "official." In the depths of behavioral ideology accumulate those contradictions which, once having reached a certain threshold, ultimately burst asunder the system of the official ideology. But, on the whole, we may say that behavioral ideology relates just as much to the socioeconomic basis and is subject to the same laws of development as ideological superstructures in the proper sense of the term. Therefore, the methods for its study should be, as already stated, basically the same methods, only somewhat differentiated and modified in accordance with the special nature of the material.

Let us now return to those "psychical" conflicts upon which psychoanalysis is based and which psychoanalysis attempts to explain in terms of a struggle between the conscious and the unconscious. From an objective point of view, all these conflicts are played out in the element of inner and outward speech (in addition, of course, to their purely physiological aspect), that is to say, they are played out in the element of behavioral ideology. They are not "psychical" but ideological conflicts and, therefore, they cannot be understood within the narrow confines of the individual organism and the individual psyche. They not only go beyond the conscious, as Freud believes, they also go beyond the individual as a whole.

Dream, myth, joke, witticism, and all the verbal components of the pathological formations reflect the struggle of various ideological tendencies and trends that take shape within *behavioral ideology*.

Those areas of behavioral ideology that correspond to Freud's official, "censored" conscious express the most steadfast and the governing factors of class consciousness. They lie close to the formulated, fully fledged ideology of the class in question, its law, its morality, its world outlook. On these levels of behavioral ideology, inner speech comes easily to order and freely turns into outward speech or, in any case, has no fear of becoming outward speech.

Other levels, corresponding to Freud's unconscious, lie at a great distance from the stable system of the ruling ideology. They bespeak the disintegration of the unity and integrity of the system, the vulnerability of the usual ideological motivations. Of course, instances of the accumulation of such inner motives— ones that erode the unity of behavioral ideology—can bear an incidental character and testify merely to the *assumption of a social déclassé status* on the part of separate individuals, but more often they testify to the emergent disintegration if not of the class as a whole then of certain of its groups. *In a healthy community and in a socially healthy personality, behavioral ideology, founded on the socioeconomic basis, is strong and sound*—here, there is no discrepancy between the official and the unofficial conscious.

The content and composition of the unofficial levels of behavioral ideology (in Freudian terms, the content and composition of the unconscious) are conditioned by historical time and class to the same degree as are its levels "under censorship" and its systems of formulated ideology (morality, law, world outlook). For example, the homosexual inclinations of an ancient Hellene of the ruling class produced absolutely no conflicts in his behavioral ideology; they freely emerged into outward speech and even found formulated ideological expression (e.g., Plato's *Symposium*).

All those conflicts with which psychoanalysis deals are characteristic in the highest degree for the European petite bourgeoisie of modern times. Freud's "censorship" very distinctly reflects the behavioral-ideological point of view of a petit bourgeois, and for that reason a somewhat comical effect is produced when Freudians transfer that point of view to the psyche of an ancient Greek or a medieval peasant. The monstrous overestimation on Freudianism's part of the sexual factor is also exceedingly revealing against the background of the present disintegration of the bourgeois family.

The wider and deeper the breach between the official and the unofficial conscious, the more difficult it becomes for motives of inner speech to turn into outward speech (oral or written or printed, in a circumscribed or broad social milieu) wherein they might acquire formulation, clarity, and rigor. Motives under these conditions begin to fail, to lose their verbal countenance, and little by little really do turn into a "foreign body" in the psyche. Whole sets of organic manifestations come, in this way, to be excluded from the zone of verbalized behavior and may become *asocial*. Thereby the sphere of the "animalian" in man enlarges.

Of course, not every area of human behavior is subject to so complete a divorce from verbal ideological formulation. After all, neither is it true that every motive in contradiction with the official ideology must degenerate into indistinct inner speech and then die out—it might well engage in a struggle with that official ideology. If such a motive *is founded on the economic being of the whole group*, if it is not merely the motive of a déclassé loner, then it has a chance for a future and perhaps even a victorious future. There is no reason why such a motive should become asocial and lose contact with communication. Only, at first a motive of this sort will develop within a small social milieu and will depart into the underground—not the psychological underground of re-pressed complexes, but the salutary political underground. That is exactly how a *revolutionary ideology* in all spheres of culture comes about.

There is one other extremely important area of human behavior in which verbal connections are put in order with great difficulty and which, therefore, is especially liable to fall out of social context, lose its ideological formulatedness, and degenerate into an aboriginal, animalian state. This is the area of *the sexual*. The disintegration of an official ideology is reflected first and foremost in this area of human behavior. It becomes the center for the accumulation of asocial and antisocial forces.

This area of human private life is preeminently the one most easily made the base for social deviations. The sexual "pair," as a sort of *social minimum*, is most easily isolated and transformed into a microcosm without the need for anything or anybody else.

All periods of social decline and disintegration are characterized by *overesti-mation of the sexual* in life and in ideology, and what is more, of the sexual in an extreme unidimensional conception; its *asocial* aspect, taken in isolation, is advanced to the forefront. The sexual aims at becoming a surrogate for the social. All human beings are divided above all into males and females. All the remaining subdivisions are held to be inessential. Only those social relations that can be sexualized are meaningful and valuable. Everything else becomes null and void.

The present day success of Freudianism throughout Europe bespeaks the complete disintegration of the *official ideological system*. A "behavioral ideol-ogy" has supervened that is turned in upon itself, disjointed, unformulated. Each aspect of life, each happening and object, goes out of kilter with a smoothly operating and universally respected context of *class and social values*. Each thing, as it were, turns its sexual, not its social, side to the human gaze. Behind every word in a poetic or philosophical text glares some stark sexual symbol. All other aspects of words, and especially the social-historical values inherent in them, cease to be heard by a modern European bourgeois—they have become merely overtones to the basic note of sexuality.

An extremely indicative and immensely interesting feature of Freudianism is its *wholesale sexualization of the family* and all family relationships in toto (the Oedipus complex). The family, that castle and keep of capitalism, evidently has become a thing economically and socially little understood and little taken to heart; and that is what has brought on its wholesale sexualization, as if thereby it were made newly meaningful or "made strange" as our formalists would say.[1] The Oedipus complex is indeed a magnificent way of making the family unit "strange." The father is not the entrepreneur, and the son is not his heir—the father is only the mother's lover, and his son is his rival!

Precisely this novel and piquant "meaningfulness," imparted to all those aspects of life that have lost their meaning, is what has attracted so broad a public to Freudianism. The obviousness and certitude of sexual drives contrast here with the ambiguity and uncertainty of all other social ideological values. Sexuality is declared the supreme criterion of *reality*, of essentiality. And the more déclassé a person is, the more keenly he senses his "naked naturalness," his "elementalness."

Freudianism—the psychology of the déclassés—is becoming the acknowledged ideological persuasion of the widest strata of the European bourgeoisie. Here is a fact profoundly symptomatic and indicative for anybody who wishes to grasp the spirit of Europe today.

The basic aspiration of the philosophy of our time is *to create a world beyond the social and the historical*. The "cosmism" of Steiner's anthroposophy, the "biologism" of Bergson, and, finally, the "psychobiologism" and "sexualism" of Freud that we have examined here—all these three trends, sharing the entire bourgeois world among them, have, each in its own way, served the aspiration of the latest philosophy. They have endowed with their own features the physiognomy of the modern *Kulturmensch*—the Steinerian, the Bergsonian, the Freudian—and they have raised the *three altars* of his belief and veneration— *Magic, Instinct* and *Sex*. Where the creative paths of history are closed, there remain only the blind alleys of the individual "livings out" of a life bereft of meaning.

---

[1] "Making strange" (*ostranenie*) is a verbal device whereby an ordinary and familiar thing is made to appear new and strange. [On the Russian formalist notion of *ostranenie*, see V. Erlich, *Russian Formalism (History-Doctrine)* (The Hague, 1955) pp. 150-151; on the formalists and Vološinov's position in their regard, see pp. 96—97 of this book and Appendix 2 in V. N. Vološinov, *Marxism and the Philosophy of Language* (New York and London; Seminar Press 1973), especially pp. 175-180. *Translator*]

APPENDIX I

Discourse in Life and Discourse in Art
(Concerning Sociological Poetics)

V. N. Vološinov

I

In the study of literature, the sociological method has been applied almost exclusively for treating historical questions while remaining virtually untouched with regard to the problems of so-called *theoretical poetics*—that whole area of issues involving artistic form and its various factors, style, and so forth.

A fallacious view, but one adhered to even by certain Marxists, has it that the sociological method becomes legitimate only at that point where poetic form acquires added complexity through the ideological factor (the content) and begins to develop historically in conditions of external social reality. Form in and of itself, according to this view, possesses its own special, not sociological but specifically artistic, nature and system of governance.

Such a view fundamentally contradicts the very bases of the Marxist method—its monism and its historicity. The consequence of this and similar views is that form and content, theory and history, are rent asunder.

But we cannot dismiss these fallacious views without further, more detailed inquiry; they are too characteristic for the whole of the modern study of the arts.

The most patent and consistent development of the point of view in question appeared recently in a work by Professor P. N. Sakulin.[1] Sakulin distinguishes two dimensions in literature and its history: the immanent and the causal. The immanent "artistic core" of literature possesses special structure and governance peculiar to itself alone; so endowed, it is capable of autonomous evolutionary

---

[1] P. N. Sakulin, *Sociologičeskij metod v literaturovedenii* [The Sociological Method in the Study of Literature] (1925).

development "by nature." But in the process of this development, literature becomes subject to the "causal" influence of the extraartistic social milieu. With the "immanent core" of literature, its structure and autonomous evolution, the sociologist can have nothing to do—those topics fall within the exclusive competence of theoretical and historical poetics and their special methods.[2] The sociological method can successfully study only the causal interaction between literature and its surrounding extraartistic social milieu. Moreover, immanent (nonsociological) analysis of the essence of literature, including its intrinsic, autonomous governance, must precede sociological analysis.[3]

Of course, no Marxist sociologist could agree with such an assertion. Nevertheless, it has to be admitted that sociology, up to the present moment, has dealt almost exclusively with concrete issues in history of literature and has not made a single serious attempt to utilize its methods in the study of the so-called "immanent" structure of a work of art. That structure has, in plain fact, been relegated to the province of aesthetic or psychological or other methods that have nothing in common with sociology.

To verify this fact we need only examine any modern work on poetics or even on the theory of art study in general. We will not find a trace of any application of sociological categories. Art is treated as if it were nonsociological "by nature" just exactly as is the physical or chemical structure of a body. Most West European and Russian scholars of the arts make precisely this claim regarding literature and art as a whole, and on this basis persistently defend the study of art as a special discipline against sociological approaches of any kind.

They motivate this claim of theirs in approximately the following way. Every item that becomes the object of supply and demand, that is, that becomes a commodity, is subject, as concerns its value and its circulation within human society, to the governing socioeconomic laws. Let us suppose that we know those laws very well; still, despite that fact, we shall understand exactly nothing

---

[2] "Elements of poetic form (sound, word, image, rhythm, composition, genre), poetic thematics, artistic style in totality—all these things are studied, as preliminary matters, with the help of methods that have been worked out by theoretical poetics, grounded in psychology, aesthetics, and linguistics, and that are now practiced in particular by the so-called formal method." *Ibid.*, p. 27.

[3] "Viewing literature as a social phenomenon, we inevitably arrive at the question of its causal conditioning. For us this is a matter of sociological causality. Only at the present time has the historian of literature received the right to assume the position of a sociologist and to pose 'why' questions so as to include literary facts within the general process of the social life of some particular period and so as to, thereupon, define the place of literature in the whole movement of history. It is at this point that the sociological method, as applied to history of literature, becomes a historical-sociological method.

In the first, immanent stage, a work was conceived of as an artistic value and not in its social and historical meaning." *Ibid.*, pp. 27, 28.

about the physical and chemical structure of the item in question. On the contrary, the study of commodities is itself in need of preliminary physical and chemical analysis of the given commodity. And the only persons competent to perform such analysis are physicists and chemists with the help of the specific methods of their fields. In the opinion of these art scholars, art stands in an analogous position. Art, too, once it becomes a social factor and becomes subject to the influence of other, likewise social, factors, takes its place, of course, within the overall system of sociological governance—but from that governance we shall never be able to derive art's *aesthetic essence*, just as we cannot derive the chemical formula for this or that commodity from the governing economic laws of commodity circulation. What art study and theoretical poetics are supposed to do is to seek such a formula for a work of art—one that is *specific* to art and independent of sociology.

This conception of the essence of art is, as we have said, fundamentally in contradiction with the bases of Marxism. To be sure, you will never find a chemical formula by the sociological method, but a scientific "formula" for any domain of *ideology* can be found, and can only be found, by the methods of sociology. All the other—"immanent"—methods are heavily involved in subjectivism and have been unable, to the present day, to break free of the fruitless controversy of opinions and points of view and, therefore, are least of all capable of finding anything even remotely resembling the rigorous and exact formulas of chemistry. Neither, of course, can the Marxist method claim to provide such a "formula"; the rigor and exactness of the natural sciences are impossible within the domain of ideological study due to the very nature of what it studies. But the closest approximation to genuine scientificness in the study of ideological creativity has become possible for the first time thanks to the sociological method in its Marxist conception. Physical and chemical bodies or substances exist outside human society as well as within it, but all products of ideological creativity arise in and for human society. Social definitions are not applicable from outside, as is the case with bodies and substances in nature—*ideological formations are intrinsically, immanently sociological.* No one is likely to dispute that point with respect to political and juridical forms—what possible nonsociological, immanent property could be found in them? The most subtle formal nuances of a law or of a political system are all equally amenable to the sociological method and only to it. But exactly the same thing is true for other ideological forms. They are all *sociological through and through*, even though their structure, mutable and complex as it is, lends itself to exact analysis only with enormous difficulty.

Art, too, is just as immanently social; the extraartistic social milieu, affecting art from outside, finds direct, intrinsic response within it. This is not a case of one foreign element affecting another but of one social formation affecting another social formation. The *aesthetic*, just as the juridical or the cognitive, is *only a variety of the social.* Theory of art, consequently, can only be a *sociology of art.*[4] No "immanent" tasks are left in its province.

II

If sociological analysis is to be properly and productively applied to the theory of art (poetics in particular), then two fallacious views that severely narrow the scope of art by operating exclusively with certain isolated factors must be rejected.

The first view can be defined as the *fetishization of the artistic work artifact.* This fetishism is the prevailing attitude in the study of art at the present time. The field of investigation is restricted to the work of art itself, which is analyzed in such a way as if everything in art were exhausted by it alone. The creator of the work and the work's contemplators remain outside the field of investigation.

The second point of view, conversely, restricts itself to the study of the psyche of the creator or of the contemplator (more often than not, it simply equates the two). For it, all art is exhausted by the experiences of the person doing the contemplating or doing the creating.

Thus, for the one point of view the object of study is only the structure of the work artifact, while for the other it is only the individual psyche of the creator or contemplator.

The first point of view advances the material to the forefront of aesthetic investigation. Form, understood very narrowly as the form of the material—that which organizes it into a single unified and complete artifact—becomes the main and very nearly exclusive object of study.

A variety of the first point of view is the so-called formal method. For the formal method, a poetic work is verbal material organized by form in some particular way. Moreover, it takes *the verbal* not as a sociological phenomenon but from an abstract linguistic point of view. That it should adopt just such a point of view is quite understandable: Verbal discourse, taken in the broader sense as a phenomenon of cultural communication, ceases to be something self-contained and can no longer be understood independently of the social situation that engenders it.

The first point of view cannot be consistently followed out to the end. The problem is that if one remains within the confines of the artifact aspect of art, there is no way of indicating even such things as the boundaries of the material or which of its features have artistic significance. The material in and of itself

---

[4] We make a distinction between theory and history of art only as a matter of a technical division of labor. There cannot be any methodological breach between them. Historical categories are of course applicable in absolutely all the fields of the humanities, whether they be historical or theoretical ones.

directly merges with the extraartistic milieu surrounding it and has an infinite number of aspects and definitions—in terms of mathematics, physics, chemistry, and so forth as well as of linguistics. However far we go in analyzing all the properties of the material and all the possible combinations of those properties, we shall never be able to find their aesthetic significance unless we slip in the contraband of another point of view that does not belong within the framework of analysis of the material. Similarly, however far we go in analyzing the chemical structure of a body or substance, we shall never understand its value and significance as a commodity unless we draw economics into the picture.

The attempt of the second view to find the aesthetic in the individual psyche of the creator or contemplator is equally vain. To continue our economic analogy, we might say that such a thing is similar to the attempt to analyze the individual psyche of a proletarian in order thereby to disclose the objective production relations that determine his position in society.

In the final analysis, both points of view are guilty of the same fault: *They attempt to discover the whole in the part,* that is, they take the structure of a part, abstractly divorced from the whole, and claim it as the structure of the whole. Meanwhile, "the artistic" in its total integrity is not located in the artifact and not located in the separately considered psyches of creator and contemplator; it encompasses all three of these factors. It is a *special form of interrelationship between creator and contemplator fixed in a work of art.*

This *artistic communication* stems from the basis common to it and other social forms, but, at the same time, it retains, as do all other forms, its own uniqueness; it is a special type of communication, possessing a form of its own peculiar to itself. *To understand this special form of social communication realized and fixed in the material of a work of art—that precisely is the task of sociological poetics.*

A work of art, viewed outside this communication and independently of it, is simply a physical artifact or an exercise in linguistics. It becomes art only in the process of the interaction between creator and contemplator, as the essential factor in this interaction. Everything in the material of a work of art that cannot be drawn into the communication between creator and contemplator, that cannot become the "medium," the means of their communication, cannot be the recipient of artistic value, either.

Those methods that ignore the social essence of art and attempt to find its nature and distinguishing features only in the organization of the work artifact are in actuality obliged to project the social interrelationship of creator and contemplator into various aspects of the material and into various devices for structuring the material. In exactly the same way, psychological aesthetics projects the same social relations into the individual psyche of the perceiver. This projection distorts the integrity of these interrelationships and gives a false picture of both the material and the psyche.

Aesthetic communication, fixed in a work of art, is, as we have already said, entirely unique and irreducible to other types of ideological communication such as the political, the juridical, the moral, and so on. If political communication establishes corresponding institutions and, at the same time, juridical forms, aesthetic communication organizes only a work of art. If the latter rejects this task and begins to aim at creating even the most transitory of political organizations or any other ideological form, then by that very fact it ceases to be aesthetic communication and relinquishes its unique character. *What characterizes aesthetic communication is the fact that it is wholly absorbed in the creation of a work of art, and in its continuous re-creations in the co-creation of contemplators, and does not require any other kind of objectification.* But, needless to say, this unique form of communication does not exist *in isolation*; it participates in the unitary flow of social life, it reflects the common economic basis, and it engages in interaction and exchange with other forms of communication.

The purpose of the present study is to try to reach an understanding of the poetic utterance as a form of this special, verbally implemented aesthetic communication. But in order to do so, we must first analyze in detail certain aspects of verbal utterances outside the realm of art—utterances in the *speech of everyday life and behavior*, for in such speech are already embedded the bases, the potentialities of artistic form. Moreover, the social essence of verbal discourse stands out here in sharper relief and the connection between an utterance and the surrounding social milieu lends itself more easily to analysis.

III

In life, verbal discourse is clearly not self-sufficient. It arises out of an extraverbal pragmatic situation and maintains the closest possible connection with that situation. Moreover, such discourse is directly informed by life itself and cannot be divorced from life without losing its import.

The kind of characterizations and evaluations of pragmatic, behavioral utterances we are likely to make are such things as: "that's a lie," "that's the truth," "that's a daring thing to say," "you can't say that," and so on and so forth.

All these and similar evaluations, whatever the criteria that govern them (ethical, cognitive, political, or other), take in a good deal more than what is enclosed within the strictly verbal (linguistic) factors of the utterance. *Together with the verbal factors, they also take in the extraverbal situation of the utterance.* These judgements and evaluations refer to a certain whole wherein the verbal discourse directly engages an event in life and merges with that event, forming an indissoluble unity. The verbal discourse itself, taken in isolation as a purely linguistic phenomenon, cannot, of course, be true or false, daring or diffident.

How does verbal discourse in life relate to the extraverbal situation that has engendered it? Let us analyze this matter, using an intentionally simplified example for the purpose.

Two people are sitting in a room. They are both silent. Then one of them says, "Well!" The other does not respond.

For us, as outsiders, this entire "conversation" is utterly incomprehensible. Taken in isolation, the utterance "Well!" is empty and unintelligible. Nevertheless, this peculiar colloquy of two persons, consisting of only one—although, to be sure, one expressively intoned—word, does make perfect sense, is fully meaningful and complete.

In order to disclose the sense and meaning of this colloquy, we must analyze it. But what is it exactly that we can subject to analysis? Whatever pains we take with the purely verbal part of the utterance, however subtly we define the phonetic, morphological, and semantic factors of the word *well*, we shall still not come a single step closer to an understanding of the whole sense of the colloquy.

Let us suppose that the intonation with which this word was pronounced is known to us: indignation and reproach moderated by a certain amount of humor. This intonation somewhat fills in the semantic void of the adverb *well* but still does not reveal the meaning of the whole.

What is it we lack, then? We lack the "extraverbal context" that made the word *well* a meaningful locution for the listener. This *extraverbal context* of the utterance is comprised of three factors: (1) the *common spatial purview* of the interlocutors (the unity of the visible—in this case, the room, the window, and so on), (2) the interlocutors' *common knowledge and understanding of the situation*, and (3) their *common evaluation* of that situation.

At the time the colloquy took place, both interlocutors *looked up* at the window and *saw* that it had begun to snow; *both knew* that it was already May and that it was high time for spring to come; finally, *both* were *sick and tired* of the protracted winter—*they both were looking forward* to spring and *both were bitterly disappointed* by the late snowfall. On this "jointly seen" (snowflakes outside the window), "jointly known" (the time of year—May) and "unanimously evaluated" (winter wearied of, spring looked forward to)—on all this the utterance *directly depends*, all this is seized in its actual, living import—is its very sustenance. And yet all this remains without verbal specification or articulation. The snowflakes remain outside the window; the date, on the page of a calendar; the evaluation, in the psyche of the speaker; and nevertheless, all this is *assumed* in the word *well*.

Now that we have been let in on the "assumed," that is, now that we know the *shared spatial and ideational purview*, the whole sense of the utterance "Well!" is perfectly clear to us and we also understand its intonation.

How does the extraverbal purview relate to the verbal discourse, how does the said relate to the unsaid?

First of all, it is perfectly obvious that, in the given case, the discourse does not at all reflect the extraverbal situation in the way a mirror reflects an object. Rather, the discourse here *resolves the situation*, bringing it to an *evaluative conclusion*, as it were. Far more often, behavioral utterances actively continue and develop a situation, adumbrate a plan for future action, and organize that action. But for us it is another aspect of the behavioral utterance that is of special importance: Whatever kind it be, the behavioral utterance always joins the participants in the situation together as *co-participants* who know, understand, and evaluate the situation in like manner. *The utterance*, consequently, *depends on their real, material appurtenance to one and the same segment of being and gives this material commonness ideological expression and further ideological development.*

Thus, the extraverbal situation is far from being merely the external cause of an utterance—it does not operate on the utterance from outside, as if it were a mechanical force. Rather, *the situation enters into the utterance as an essential constitutive part of the structure of its import.* Consequently, a behavioral utterance as a meaningful whole is comprised of two parts: (1) the part realized or actualized in words and (2) the assumed part. On this basis, the behavioral utterance can be liked to the enthymeme.[5]

However, it is an enthymeme of a special order. The very term enthymeme (literally translated from the Greek, something located in the heart or mind) sounds a bit too psychological. One might be led to think of the situation as something in the mind of the speaker on the order of a subjective-psychical act (a thought, idea, feeling). But that is not the case. The individual and subjective are backgrounded here by *the social and objective*. What *I* know, see, want, love, and so on cannot be assumed. Only what all of us speakers know, see, love, recognize—only those points on which we are all united can become the assumed part of an utterance. Furthermore, this fundamentally social phenomenon is completely objective; it consists, above all, of *the material unity of world that enters the speakers' purview* (in our example, the room, the snow outside the window, and so on) and of *the unity of the real conditions of life* that generate a *community of value judgements*—the speakers' belonging to the same family, profession, class, or other social group, and their belonging to the same time period (the speakers are, after all, contemporaries). Assumed value judgements are, therefore, not individual emotions but regular and essential social acts. *Individual* emotions can come into play only as *overtones* accompanying the *basic tone of social evaluation.* "I" can realize itself verbally only on the basis of "we."

[5]The enthymeme is a form of syllogism one of whose premises is not expressed but assumed. For example: "Socrates is a man, therefore he is mortal." The assumed premise: "All men are mortal."

Thus, every utterance in the business of life is an objective social enthymeme. It is something like a "password" known only to those who belong to the same social purview. The distinguishing characteristic of behavioral utterances consists precisely in the fact that they make myriad connections with the extraverbal context of life and, once severed from that context, lose almost all their import—a person ignorant of the immediate pragmatic context will not understand these utterances.

This immediate context may be of varying scope. In our example, the context is extremely narrow: It is *circumscribed by the room and the moment of occurrence,* and the utterance makes an intelligible statement only for the two persons involved. However, the unified purview on which an utterance depends can expand in both space and time: *The "assumed" may be that of the family, clan, nation, class and may encompass days or years or whole epochs.* The wider the overall purview and its corresponding social group, the more *constant* the assumed factors in an utterance become.

When the assumed real purview of an utterance is narrow, when, as in our example, it coincides with the actual purview of two people sitting in the same room and seeing the same thing, then even the most momentary change within that purview can become the assumed. Where the purview is wider, the utterance can operate only on the basis of constant, stable factors in life and substantive, fundamental social evaluations.

Especially great importance, in this case, belongs to assumed evaluations. The fact is that all the basic social evaluations that stem directly from the distinctive characteristics of the given social group's economic being are usually not articulated: They have entered the flesh and blood of all representatives of the group; they organize behavior and actions; they have merged, as it were, with the objects and phenomena to which they correspond, and for that reason they are in no need of special verbal formulation. We seem to perceive the value of a thing together with its being as one of its qualities, we seem, for instance, to sense, along with its warmth and light, the sun's value for us, as well. All the phenomena that surround us are similarly merged with value judgments. If a value judgment is in actual fact conditioned by the being of a given community, it becomes a matter of dogmatic belief, something taken for granted and not subject to discussion. On the contrary, whenever some basic value judgment is verbalized and justified, we may be certain that if has already become dubious, has separated from its referent, has ceased to organize life, and, consequently, has lost its connection with the existential conditions of the given group.

A health social value judgment remains within life and from that position organizes the very form of an utterance and its intonation, but it does not at all aim to find suitable expression in the content side of discourse. Once a value judgment shifts from formal factors to content, we may be sure that a reevaluation is in the offing. Thus, a viable value judgment exists wholly without incorporation into the content of discourse and is not derivable therefrom; instead, it determines the *very selection of the verbal material and the form of the verbal whole*. It finds its purest expression in *intonation*. Intonation establishes a firm link between verbal discourse and the extraverbal context—genuine, living intonation moves verbal discourse beyond the border of the verbal, so to speak.

Let us stop to consider in somewhat greater detail the connection between intonation and the pragmatic context of life in the example utterance we have been using. This will allow us to make a number of important observations about the social nature of intonation.

IV

First of all, we must emphasize that the word *well*—a word virtually empty semantically—cannot to any extent predetermine intonation through its own content. Any intonation—joyful, sorrowful, contemptuous, and so on—can freely and easily operate in this word; it all depends on the context in which the word appears. In our example, the context determining the intonation used (indignant-reproachful but moderated by humor) is provided entirely by the extraverbal situation that we have already analyzed, since, in this instance, there is no immediate verbal context. We might say in advance that even were such an immediate verbal context present and even, moreover, if that context were entirely sufficient from all other points of view, the intonation would still take us beyond its confines. Intonation can be thoroughly understood only when one is in touch with the assumed value judgments of the given social group, whatever the scope of that group might be. *Intonation always lies on the border of the verbal and the nonverbal, the said and the unsaid*. In intonation, discourse comes directly into contact with life. And it is in intonation above all that the speaker comes into contact with the listener or listeners—intonation is social par excellence. It is especially sensitive to all the vibrations in the social atmosphere surrounding the speaker.

The intonation in our example stemmed from the interlocutors' shared yearning for spring and shared disgruntlement over the protracted winter. This commonness of evaluations assumed between them supplied the basis for the intonation, the basis for the distinctness and certitude of its major tonality. Given an atmosphere of sympathy, the intonation could freely undergo deployment and differentiation within the range of the major tone. But if there were no such firmly dependable "choral support," the intonation would have gone in a different direction and taken on different tones—perhaps those of provocation or annoyance with the listener, or perhaps the intonation would simply have contracted and been reduced to the minimum. When a person anticipates the disagreement of his interlocutor or, at any rate, is uncertain or doubtful of his agreement, he intones his words differently. We shall see later that not only intonation but the whole formal structure of speech depends to a significant degree on what the relation of the utterance is to the assumed community of values belonging to the social milieu wherein the discourse figures. A creatively productive, assured, and rich intonation is possible only on the basis of presupposed "choral support." Where such support is lacking, the voice falters and its intonational richness is reduced, as happens, for instance, when a person laughing suddenly realizes that he is laughing alone—his laughter either ceases or degenerates, becomes forced, loses its assurance and clarity and its ability to generate joking and amusing talk. *The commonness of assumed basic value judgments constitutes the canvas upon which living human speech embroiders the designs of intonation.*

Intonation's set toward possible sympathy, toward "choral support," does not exhaust its social nature. It is only one side of intonation—the side turned toward the listener. But intonation contains yet another extremely important factor for the sociology of discourse.

If we scrutinize the intonation of our example, we will notice that it has one "mysterious" feature requiring special explanation.

In point of fact, the intonation of the word *well* voiced not only passive dissatisfaction with an occurring event (the snowfall) but also active indignation and reproach. To whom is this reproach addressed? Clearly not to the listener but to somebody else. This tack of the intonational movement patently makes an opening in the situation for a *third participant*. Who is this third participant? Who is the recipient of the reproach? The snow? Nature? Fate, perhaps?

Of course, in our simplified example of a behavioral utterance the third participant—the "hero" of this verbal production—has not yet assumed full and definitive shape; the intonation has demarcated a definite place for the hero but his semantic equivalent has not been supplied and he remains nameless. Intonation has established an active attitude toward the referent, toward the object of the utterance, an attitude of a kind verging on *apostrophe* to that object as the incarnate, living culprit, while the listener—the second participant—is, as it were, called in *as witness and ally*.

Almost any example of live intonation in emotionally charged behavioral speech proceeds as if it addressed, behind inanimate objects and phenomena, animate participants and agents in life; in other words, it has an inherent *tendency toward personification*. If the intonation is not held in check, as in our example, by a certain amount of irony, then it becomes the source of the mythological image, the incantation, the prayer, as was the case in the earliest stages of culture. In our case, however, we have to do with an extremely important phenomenon of language creativity—*the intonational metaphor*: The intonation of the utterance "Well!" makes the word sound as if it were reproaching the living culprit of the late snowfall—winter. We have in our example an instance of *pure* intonational metaphor wholly confined within the intonation; but latent within it, in cradle, so to speak, there exists the possibility of the usual *semantic metaphor*. Were this possibility to be realized, the word *well* would expand into some such metaphorical expression as: "What a *stubborn winter! It just won't give up*, though goodness knows it's time!" But this possibility, inherent in the intonation, remained unrealized and the utterance made do with the almost semantically inert adverb *well*.

It should be noted that the intonation in behavioral speech, on the whole, is a great deal more metaphorical than the words used: The aboriginal myth-making spirit seems to have remained alive in it. Intonation makes it sound as if the world surrounding the speaker were still full of animate forces—it threatens and rails against or adores and cherishes inanimate objects and phenomena, whereas the usual metaphors of colloquial speech for the most part have been effaced and the words become semantically spare and prosaic.

Close kinship unites the intonational metaphor with the *gesticulatory metaphor* (indeed, words were themselves originally lingual gestures constituting one component of a complex, omnicorporeal gesture)—the term "gesture" being understood here in a broad sense including miming as facial gesticulation. Gesture, just as intonation, requires the choral support of surrounding persons; only in an atmosphere of sympathy is free and assured gesture possible. Furthermore, and again just as intonation, gesture makes an opening in the situation and introduces a third participant—the hero. Gesture always has latent within itself the germ of attack or defence, of threat or caress, with the contemplator and listener relegated to the role of ally or witness. Often, the "hero" is merely some inanimate thing, some occurrence or circumstance in life. How often we shake our fist at "someone" in a fit of temper or simply scowl at empty space, and there is literally nothing we cannot smile at—the sun, trees, thoughts.

A point that must constantly be kept in mind (something that psychological aesthetics often forgets to do) is this: *Intonation and gesture are active and objective by tendency*. They not only express the passive mental state of the speaker but also always have embedded in them a living, forceful relation with the external world and with the social milieu—enemies, friends, allies. When a person intones and gesticulates, he assumes an active social position with respect to certain specific values, and this position is conditioned by the very bases of his social being. It is precisely this objective and sociological, and not subjective and psychological, aspect of intonation and gesture that should interest theorists of the various relevant arts, inasmuch as it is here that reside forces in the arts that are responsible for aesthetic creativity and that devise and organize artistic form.

As we see then, every instance of intonation is oriented *in two directions*: with respect to the listener as ally or witness and with respect to the object of the utterance as the third, living participant whom the intonation scolds or caresses, denigrates or magnifies. *This double social orientation is what determines all aspects of intonation and makes it intelligible.* And this very same thing is true for all the other factors of verbal utterances: They are all organized and in every way given shape in the same process of the speaker's *double orientation*; this social origin is only most easily detectable in intonation since it is the verbal factor of greatest sensitivity, elasticity, and freedom.

Thus, as we now have a right to claim, *any locution actually said aloud or written down for intelligible communication* (i.e., anything but words merely reposing in a dictionary) *is the expression and product of the social interaction of three participants: the speaker* (author), *the listener* (reader), and *the topic* (the who or what) *of speech* (the hero). Verbal discourse is a social event; it is not self-contained in the sense of some abstract linguistic quantity, nor can it be derived psychologically from the speaker's subjective consciousness taken in isolation. Therefore, both the formal linguistic approach and the psychological approach equally miss the mark: The concrete, sociological essence of verbal discourse, that which alone can make it true or false, banal or distinguished, necessary or unnecessary, remains beyond the ken and reach of both these points of view. Needless to say, it is also this very same "social soul" of verbal discourse that makes it beautiful or ugly, that is, that makes it artistically meaningful, as well. To be sure, once subordinated to the basic and more concrete sociological approach, both abstract points of view—the formal linguistic and the psychological—retain their value. Their collaboration is even absolutely indispensable; but separately, each by itself in isolation, they are inert.

The concrete utterance (and not the linguistic abstraction) is born, lives, and dies in the process of social interaction between the participants of the utterance. Its form and meaning are determined basically by the form and character of this interaction. When we cut the utterance off from the real grounds that nurture it, we lose the key to its form as well as to its import—all we have left is an abstract linguistic shell or an equally abstract semantic scheme (the banal "idea of the work" with which earlier theorists and historians of literature dealt)—two abstractions that are not mutually joinable because there are no concrete grounds for their organic synthesis.

It remains for us now only to sum up our short analysis of utterance in life and of those *artistic potentials, those rudiments of future form and content*, that we have detected in it.

The meaning and import of an utterance in life (of whatever particular kind that utterance may be) do not coincide with the purely verbal composition of the utterance. Articulated words are impregnated with assumed and unarticulated qualities. What are called the "understanding" and "evaluation" of an utterance (agreement or disagreement) always encompass the extraverbal pragmatic situation together with the verbal discourse proper. Life, therefore, does not affect an utterance from without; it penetrates and exerts an influence on an utterance from within, as that unity and commonness of being surrounding the speakers and that unity and commonness of essential social value judgments issuing from that being without all of which no intelligible utterance is possible. Intonation lies on the border between life and the verbal aspect of the utterance; it, as it were, pumps energy from a life situation into the verbal discourse, it endows everything linguistically stable with living historical momentum and uniqueness. Finally, the utterance reflects the social interaction of the speaker, listener, and hero as the product and fixation in verbal material of the act of living communication among them.

Verbal discourse is like a *"scenario"* of a certain event. A viable understanding of the whole import of discourse must *reproduce* this event of the mutual relationship between speakers, must, as it were, "reenact" it, with the person wishing to understand taking upon himself the role of the listener. But in order to carry out that role, he must distinctly understand the positions of the other two participants, as well.

For the linguistic point of view, neither this event nor its living participants exist, of course; the linguistic point of view deals with abstract, bare words and their equally abstract components (phonetic, morphological, and so on). Therefore, the *total import of discourse* and *its ideological value*—the cognitive, political, aesthetic, or other—are inaccessible to it. Just as there cannot be a linguistic logic or a linguistic politics, so there cannot be a linguistic poetics.

V

In what way does an artistic verbal utterance—a complete work of poetic art—differ from an utterance in the business of life?

It is immediately obvious that discourse in art neither is nor can be so closely dependent on all the factors of the extraverbal context, on all that is seen and known, as in life. A poetic work cannot rely on objects and events in the immediate milieu as things "understood," without making even the slightest allusion to them in the verbal part of the utterance. In this regard, a great deal more is demanded of discourse in literature: Much that could remain outside the utterance in life must find verbal representation. Nothing must be left unsaid in a poetic work from the pragmatic-referential point of view.

Does it follow from this that in literature the speaker, listener, and hero come in contact for the first time, knowing nothing about one another, having no purview in common, and are, therefore, bereft of anything on which they can jointly rely or hold assumptions about? Certain writers on these topics are inclined to think so.

But in actuality a poetic work, too, is closely enmeshed in the unarticulated context of life. If it were true that author, listener, and hero, as abstract persons, come into contact for the first time devoid of any unifying purview and that the words used are taken as from a dictionary, then it is hardly likely that even a nonpoetic work would result, and certainly not a poetic one. Science does to some degree approach this extreme—a scientific definition has a minimum of the "assumed"; but it would be possible to prove that even science cannot do entirely without the assumed.

In literature, assumed value judgments play a role of particular importance. We might say that *a poetic work is a powerful condenser of unarticulated social evaluations*—each word is saturated with them. *It is these social evaluations that organize form as their direct expression.*

Value judgments, first of all, determine the author's *selection of words* and the reception of that selection (the coselection) by the listener. The poet, after all, selects words not from the dictionary but from the context of life where words have been steeped in and become permeated with value judgments. Thus, he selects the value judgments associated with the words and does so, moreover, from the standpoint of the incarnated bearers of those value judgments. It can be said that the poet constantly works in conjunction with his listener's sympathy or antipathy, agreement or disagreement. Furthermore, evaluation is operative also with regard to the object of the utterance—the hero. The simple selection of an epithet or a metaphor is already an active evaluative act with orientation in both directions—toward the listener and toward the hero. *Listener and hero are constant participants in the creative event*, which does not for a single instant cease to be an event of living communication involving all three.

The problem of sociological poetics would be resolved if each factor of form could be explained as the active expression of evaluation in these two directions—toward the listener and toward the object of utterance, the hero.[6] But at the present time the data are too insufficient for such a task to be carried out. All that can be done is to map out at least the preliminary steps leading toward that goal.

The formalistic aesthetics of the present day defines artistic forms as *the form of the material*. If this point of view be carried out consistently, content must necessarily be ignored, since no room is left for it in the poetic work; at best, it may be regarded as a factor of the material and in that way, indirectly, be organized by artistic form in its direct bearing on the material.[7]

So understood, form loses its active evaluative character and becomes merely a stimulus of passive feelings of pleasure in the perceiver.

It goes without saying that form is realized with the help of the material—it is fixed in material; but by virtue of *its significance* it exceeds the material. *The*

---

[6] We ignore technical questions of form here but will have something to say on this topic later.

[7] The point of view of V. M. Žirmunskij.

meaning, the import of form has to do not with the material but with the content. So, for instance, the form of a statue may be said to be not the form of the marble but the form of the human body, with the added qualification that the form "heroicizes" the human depicted or "dotes upon" him or, perhaps, denigrates him (the caricature style in the plastic arts); that is, the form expresses some specific evaluation of the object depicted.

The evaluative significance of form is especially obvious in verse. Rhythm and other formal elements of verse overtly express a certain active attitude toward the object depicted: The form celebrates or laments or ridicules that object.

Psychological aesthetics calls this the "emotional factor" of form. But it is not the psychological side of the matter that is important for us, not the identity of the psychical forces that take part in the creation of form and the cocreative perception of form. What is important is the significance of these experiences, their active role, their bearing on content. Through the agency of artistic form the creator takes up *an active position with respect to content*. The form in and of itself need not necessarily be pleasurable (the hedonistic explanation of form is absurd); what it must be is a *convincing evaluation* of the content. So, for instance, while the form of "the enemy" might even be repulsive, the positive state, the pleasure that the contemplator derives in the end, is a consequence of the fact that the form is *appropriate to the enemy* and that it is *technically perfect* in its realization through the agency of the material. It is in these two aspects that form should be studied: with respect to content, as its ideological evaluation, and with respect to the material, as the technical realization of that evaluation.

The ideological evaluation expressed through form is not at all supposed to transpose into content as a maxim or a proposition of a moral, political, or other kind. The evaluation should remain in the rhythm, *in the very evaluative impetus* of the epithet or metaphor, *in the manner of the unfolding* of the depicted event; it is supposed to be realized by the formal means of the material only. But, at the same time, while not transposing into content, the form must not lose its connection with content, its correlation with it, otherwise it becomes a technical experiment devoid of any real artistic import.

The general definition of style that classical and neoclassical poetics had advanced, together with the basic division of style into "high" and "low," aptly brings out precisely this active evaluative nature of artistic form. The structure of form is indeed *hierarchical*, and in this respect it comes close to political and juridical gradations. Form similarly creates, in an artistically configured content, a complex system of hierarchical interrelations: Each of its elements—an epithet or a metaphor, for instance—either raises the designatum to a higher degree or lowers it or equalizes it. The selection of a hero or an event determines from the very outset the general level of the form and the admissibility of this or that particular set of configurating devices. And this basic requirement of *stylistic suitability* has in view *the evaluative-hierarchical suitability of form and content*: They must be *equally adequate* for one another. The selection of content and the selection of form constitute one and the same act establishing the creator's basic position; and in that act one and the same social evaluation finds expression.

VI

Sociological analysis can take its starting point only, of course, from the purely verbal, linguistic makeup of a work, but it must not and cannot confine itself within those limits, as linguistic poetics does. Artistic contemplation via the reading of a poetic work does, to be sure, start from the grapheme (the visual image of written or printed words), but at the very instant of perception this visual image gives way to and is very nearly obliterated by other verbal factors—articulation, sound image, intonation, meaning—and these factors eventually take us beyond the border of the verbal altogether. And so it can be said that *the purely linguistic factor of a work is to the artistic whole as the grapheme is to the verbal whole*. In poetry, as in life, verbal discourse is a *"scenario" of an event*. Competent artistic perception reenacts it, sensitively surmising from the words and the forms of their organization the specific, living interrelations of the author with the world he depicts and entering into those interrelations as a third participant (the listener's role). Where linguistic analysis sees only words and the interrelations of their abstract factors (phonetic, morphological, syntactic, and so on), there, for living artistic perception and for concrete sociological analysis, relations among *people* stand revealed, relations merely reflected and fixed in verbal material. Verbal discourse is the skeleton that takes on living flesh only in the process of creative perception—consequently, only in the process of living social communication.

In what follows here we shall attempt to provide a brief and preliminary sketch of the essential factors in the interrelationships of the participants in an artistic event—those factors that determine the broad and basic lines of poetic style as a social phenomenon. Any further detailing of these factors would, of course, go beyond the scope of the present essay.

The author, hero, and listener that we have been talking about all this time are to be understood not as entities outside the artistic event but only as entities of the very perception of an artistic work, entities that are essential constitutive factors of the work. They are the living forces that determine form and style and are distinctly detectable by any competent contemplator. This means that all those definitions that a historian of literature and society mighty apply to the author and his heroes—the author's biography, the precise qualifications of heroes in chronological and sociological terms and so on—are excluded here: They do not enter directly into the structure of the work but remain outside it. The listener, too, is taken here as the listener whom the author himself takes into account, the one toward whom the work is oriented and who, consequently, intrinsically determines the work's structure. Therefore, we do not at all mean the actual people who in fact made up the reading public of the author in question.

The first form-determining factor of content is the *evaluative rank* of the depicted event and its agent—the hero (whether named or not), taken in strict correlation with the rank of the creator and contemplator. Here we have to do, just as in legal or political life, with a *two-sided relationship*: master-slave, ruler-subject, comrade-comrade, and the like.

The basic stylistic tone of an utterance is therefore determined above all by who is talked about and what his relation is to the speaker—whether he is higher or lower than or equal to him on the scale of the social hierarchy. King, father, brother, slave, comrade, and so on, as heroes of an utterance, also determine its formal structure. And this *specific hierarchical weight* of the hero is determined, in its turn, by that unarticulated context of basic evaluations in which a poetic work, too, participates. Just as the "intonational metaphor" in our example utterance from life established an organic relationship with the object of the utterance, so also all elements of the style of a poetic work are permeated with the author's evaluative attitude toward content and express his basic social position. Let us stress once again that we have in mind here not those ideological evaluations that are incorporated into the content of a work in the form of judgments or conclusions but that deeper, more ingrained kind of *evaluation via form* that finds expression in the very manner in which the artistic material is viewed and deployed.

Certain languages, Japanese in particular, possess a rich and varied store of special lexical and grammatical forms to be used in strict accordance with the rank of the hero of the utterance (language etiquette).[8]

We might say that what is still a *matter of grammar* for the Japanese has already become for us a *matter of style*. The most important stylistic components of the heroic epic, the tragedy, the ode, and so forth are determined precisely by the hierarchical status of the object of the utterance with respect to the speaker.

It should not be supposed that this hierarchical interdefinition of creator and hero has been eliminated from modern literature. It has been made more complex and does not reflect the contemporary sociopolitical hierarchy with the same degree of distinctness as, say, classicism did in its time—but *the very principle of change of style in accordance with change in the social value of the hero of the utterance* certainly remains in force as before. After all, it is not his personal enemy that the poet hates, not his personal friend that his form treats

---

[8] See W. Humboldt, *Kawi-Werk* No. 2:335, and Hoffman, *Japan. Sprachlehre*, p. 75.

with love and tenderness, not the events from his private life that he rejoices or sorrows over. Even if a poet has in fact borrowed his passion in good measure from the circumstances of his own private life, still, he must *socialize* that passion and, consequently, elaborate the event with which it corresponds to the level of *social significance*.

The second style-determining factor in the interrelationship between hero and creator is *the degree of their proximity to one another*. All languages possess direct grammatical means of expression for this aspect: first, second, and third persons and variable sentence structure in accordance with the person of the subject ("I" or "you" or "he"). The form of a proposition about a third person, the form of an address to a second person, the form of an utterance about oneself (and their modifications) are already different in terms of grammar. Thus, here *the very structure of the language reflects the event of the speakers' interrelationship*.

Certain languages have purely grammatical forms capable of conveying with even greater flexibility the nuances of the speakers' social interrelationship and the various degrees of their proximity. From this angle, the so-called "inclusive" and "exclusive" forms of the plural in certain languages present a case of special interest. For example, if a speaker using the form *we* has the listener in mind and includes him in the subject of the proposition, then he uses one form, whereas if he means himself and some other person (*we* in the sense of *I* and *he*), he uses a different form. Such is the use of the dual in certain Australian languages, for instance. There, too, are found two special forms of the trial: one meaning *I and you and he;* the other, *I and he and he* (with *you*—the listener—excluded).[9]

In European languages these and similar interrelationships between speakers have no special grammatical expression. The character of these languages is more abstract and not so capable of reflecting the situation of utterance via grammatical structure. However, interrelationships between speakers do find expression in these languages—and expression of far greater subtlety and diversity—*in the style and intonation of utterances.* Here the social situation of creativity finds thoroughgoing reflection in a work by means of purely artistic devices.

The form of a poetic work is determined, therefore, in many of its factors by *how the author perceives his hero*—the hero who serves as the organizing center of the utterance. The form of *objective narration*, the form of *address or apostrophe* (prayer, hymn, certain lyric forms), the form of *self-expression* (confession, autobiography, lyric avowal—an important form of the love lyric) are determined precisely by the *degree of proximity between author and hero*.

Both the factors we have indicated—the hierarchical value of the hero and the degree of his proximity to the author—are as yet insufficient, taken indepen-

[9] See Matthews, *Aboriginal Languages of Victoria.* Also, Humboldt, *Kawi-Werk*.

dently and in isolation, for the determination of artistic form. The fact is that a third participant is constantly in play as well—the listener, whose presence affects the interrelationship of the other two (creator and hero).

The interrelationship of author and hero never, after all, actually is an intimate relationship of two; all the while form makes provision for the third participant—the listener—who exerts crucial influence on all the other factors of the work.

In what way can the listener determine the style of a poetic utterance? Here, too, we must distinguish two basic factors: first, the listener's proximity to the author and, second, his relation to the hero. Nothing is more perilous for aesthetics than to ignore the autonomous role of the listener. A very commonly held opinion has it that the listener is to be regarded as equal to the author, excepting the latter's technical performance, and that the position of a competent listener is supposed to be a simple reproduction of the author's position. In actual fact this is not so. Indeed, the opposite may sooner be said to be true: The listener never equals the author. The listener has *his own independent place* in the event of artistic creation; he must occupy a special, and, what is more, a *two-sided* position in it—with respect to the author and with respect to the hero—and it is this position that has determinative effect on the style of an utterance.

How does the author sense his listener? In our example of an utterance in the business of life, we have seen to what degree the presumed agreement or disagreement of the listener shaped an utterance. Exactly the same is true regarding all factors of form. To put it figuratively, the listener normally stands *side by side* with the author as his ally, but this classical positioning of the listener is by no means always the case.

Sometimes the listener begins to lean toward the hero of the utterance. The most unmistakable and typical expression of this is the polemical style that aligns the hero and the listener together. Satire, too, can involve the listener as someone calculated to be close to the hero ridiculed and not to the ridiculing author. This constitutes a sort of *inclusive form of ridicule* distinctly different from the exclusive form where the listener is in solidarity with the jeering author. In romanticism, an interesting phenomenon can be observed where the author *concludes an alliance*, as it were, *with his hero against the listener* (Friedrich Schlegel's *Lucinda* and, in Russian literature, *Hero of Our Time* to some extent).

Of very special character and interest for analysis is the author's sense of his listener in the forms of the confession and the autobiography. All shades of feeling from humble reverence before the listener, as before a veritable judge, to contemptuous distrust and hostility can have determinative effect on the style of a confession or an autobiography. Extremely interesting material for the illustration of this contention can be found in the works of Dostoevskij. The confessional style of

Ippolit's "article" (*The Idiot*) is determined by an almost extreme degree of contemptuous distrust and hostility directed toward all who are to hear this dying confession. Similar tones, but somewhat softened, determine the style of *Notes from Underground*. The style of "Stavrogin's Confession" (*The Possessed*) displays far greater trust in the listener and acknowledgments of his rights, although here too, from time to time, a feeling almost of hatred for the listener erupts, which is what is responsible for the jaggedness of its style. Playing the fool, as a special form of utterance, one, to be sure, lying on the periphery of the artistic, is determined above all by an extremely complex and tangled conflict of the speaker with the listener.

A form especially sensitive to the position of the listener is the lyric. The underlying condition for lyric intonation is *the absolute certainty of the listener's sympathy*. Should any doubt on this score creep into the lyric situation, the style of the lyric changes drastically. This conflict with the listener finds its most egregious expression in so-called lyric irony (Heine, and in modern poetry, Laforgue, Annenskij, and others). The form of irony in general is conditioned by a social conflict: It is the encounter in one voice of two incarnate value judgments and their interference with one another.

In modern aesthetics a special, so-called juridical theory of tragedy was proposed, a theory amounting essentially to the attempt to conceive of *the structure of a tragedy as the structure of a trial in court*.[10]

The interrelationship of hero and chorus, on the one side, and the overall position of the listener, on the other, do indeed, to a degree, lend themselves to juridical interpretation. But of course this can only be meant as *an analogy*. The important common feature of tragedy—indeed of any work of art—and judicial process comes down merely to the existence of "sides," that is, the occupying by the several participants of *different positions*. The terms, so widespread in literary terminology, that define the poet as "judge," "exposer," "witness," "defender," and even "executioner" (the phraseology for "scourging satire"— Juvenal, Barbier, Nekrasov, and others), and associated definitions for heroes and listeners, reveal by way of analogy, the same social base of poetry. At all events, author, hero, and listener nowhere merge together into one indifferent mass—they occupy *autonomous positions*, they are indeed "sides," the sides not of a judicial process but of an artistic event with specific social structure the "protocol" of which is the work of art.

It would not be amiss at this point to stress once again that we have in mind, and have had in mind all this time, the listener as an immanent participant in the artistic event who has determinative effect on the form of the work from within. This listener, on a par with the author and the hero, is an essential, intrinsic

---

[10] For the most interesting development of this point of view, see Hermann Cohen, *Ästhetik des reinen Gefühls*, vol. 2.

factor of the work and does not at all coincide with the so-called reading public, located outside the work, whose artistic tastes and demands can be consciously taken into account. Such a conscious account is incapable of direct and profound effect on artistic form in the process of its living creation. What is more, if this conscious account of the reading public does come to occupy a position of any importance in a poet's creativity, that creativity inevitably loses its artistic purity and degrades to a lower social level.

This external account bespeaks the poet's loss of *his immanent listener*, his divorce from the *social whole* that *intrinsically*, aside from all abstract considerations, has the capability of determining *his value judgments* and the artistic form of his poetic utterances, which form is the expression of those crucial social value judgments. The more a poet is cut off from the social unity of his group, the more likely he is to take into account the *external* demands of a *particular reading public*. Only a social group alien to the poet can determine his creative work from outside. One's *own* group needs no such external definition: It exists in the poet's voice, in the basic tone and intonations of that voice—whether the poet himself intends this or not.

The poet acquires his words and learns to intone them *over the course of his entire life* in the process of his every-sided contact with his environment. The poet begins to use those words and intonations already in the *inner speech* with the help of which he thinks and becomes conscious of himself, even when he does not produce utterances. It is naive to suppose that one can assimilate as one's own *an external speech that runs counter to one's inner speech*, that is, runs counter to one's whole inner verbal manner of being aware of oneself and the world. Even if it is possible to create such a thing for some pragmatic occasion, still, as something cut off from all sources of sustenance, it will be devoid of any artistic productiveness. A poet's style is engendered from *the style of his inner speech*, which does not lend itself to control, and his inner speech is itself the product of his entire social life. "Style is the man," they say; but we might say: Style is at least two persons or, more accurately, one person plus his social group in the form of its authoritative representative, the listener—the constant participant in a person's inner and outward speech.

The fact of the matter is that no conscious act of any degree of distinctness can do without inner speech, without words and intonations—without evaluations, and, consequently, every conscious act is already a social act, an act of communication. Even the most intimate self-awareness is an attempt to translate oneself into the common code, to take stock of another's point of view, and, consequently, entails orientation toward a possible listener. This listener may be only the bearer of the value judgments of the social group to which the "conscious" person belongs. In this regard, consciousness, provided that we do not lose sight of its content, is *not just a psychological phenomenon* but also, and above all, an *ideological phenomenon, a product of social intercourse.* This constant *coparticipant* in all our conscious acts determines not only the content of consciousness but also—and this is the main point for us—the very *selection* of the content, the selection of what precisely we become conscious of, and thus determines also those *evaluations* which permeate consciousness and which psychology usually calls the "emotional tone" of consciousness. It is precisely from this constant participant in all our conscious acts that the listener who determines artistic form is engendered.

There is nothing more perilous than to conceive of this subtle social structure of verbal creativity as analogous with the conscious and cynical speculations of the bourgeois publisher who "calculates the prospects of the book market," and to apply to the characterization of the immanent structure of a work categories of the "supply-demand" type. Alas, all too many "sociologists" are likely to identify the creative writer's service to society with the vocation of the enterprising publisher.

Under the conditions of the bourgeois economy, the book market does, of course, "regulate" writers, but this is not in any way to be identified with the regulative role of the listener as a constant structural element in artistic creativity. For a historian of the literature of the capitalist era, the market is a very important factor, but for theoretical poetics, which studies the basic ideological structure of art, that external factor is irrelevant. However, even in the historical study of literature the history of the book market must not be confused with the history of literature.

VII

All the form-determining factors of an artistic utterance that we have analyzed—(1) the hierarchical value of the hero or event serving as the content of the utterance, (2) the degree of the latter's proximity to the author, and (3) the listener and his interrelationship with the author, on the one side, and the hero, on the other—all those factors are *the contact points between the social forces of extraartistic reality and verbal art.* Thanks precisely to that kind of *intrinsically social structure* which artistic creation possesses, it is *open on all sides to the influence of other domains of life.* Other ideological spheres, prominently including the sociopolitical order and the economy, have determinative effect on verbal art not merely from outside but with direct bearing upon its intrinsic structural elements. And, conversely, the artistic interaction of author, listener, and hero may exert its influence on other domains of social intercourse.

Full and thoroughgoing elucidation of questions as to who the typical heroes of literature at some particular period are, what the typical formal orientation of the author toward them is, what the interrelationships of the author and hero with the listener are in the whole of an artistic creation—elucidation of such questions presupposes thoroughgoing analysis of the economic and ideological conditions of the time.

But these concrete historical issues exceed the scope of theoretical poetics which, however, still does include one other important task. Up to now we have been concerned only with those factors which determine form in its relation to content, that is, form as the embodied social evaluation of precisely that content, and we have ascertained that every factor of form is a product of social interaction. But we also pointed out that form must be understood from another angle, as well—as form realized with the help of *specific material*. This opens up a whole long series of questions connected with *the technical aspect of form*.

Of course, *these technical questions can be separated out from questions of the sociology of form only in abstract terms; in actuality* it is impossible to divorce the *artistic import* of some device, say, a metaphor that relates to content and expresses the formal evaluation of it (i.e., the metaphor degrades the object or raises it to a higher rank), from *the purely linguistic* specification of that device.

The extraverbal import of a metaphor—a regrouping of values—and *its linguistic covering*—a semantic shift—are merely different points of view on one and the same real phenomenon. But the second point of view is subordinate to the first: A poet uses a metaphor in order to regroup values and not for the sake of a linguistic exercise.

All questions of form can be taken in relation with material—in the given case, in relation with language in its linguistic conception. Technical analysis will then amount to the question as to *which linguistic means are used for the realization of the socioartistic purpose of the form*. But if that purpose is not known, if its import is not elucidated in advance, technical analysis will be absurd.

Technical questions of form, of course, go beyond the scope of the task we have set ourself here. Moreover, their treatment would require an incomparably more diversified and elaborated analysis of the socioartistic aspect of verbal art. Here we have been able to provide only a brief sketch of the basic directions such an analysis must take.

If we have succeeded in demonstrating even the mere possibility of a sociological approach to the immanent structure of poetic form, we may consider our task to have been fulfilled.

V. N. Vološinov and the
Structure of Language in Freudianism

Neal H. Bruss

Explicitly, V. N. Vološinov's critique of Freud seems to be an overearnest attempt to save Western audiences from mystification by the decadent cult ideology he takes "Freudianism" (as he calls it) to be. At this level, Vološinov is most concerned with condemning Freud's depiction of human nature as rooted in sexual instincts, rather than in social life and history, and the evocation in his work of the equally unacceptable philosophies of Schopenhauer and Nietzsche.

Such a rejection of Freudianism by Marxism is fully understandable, particularly given the inconclusiveness of the persistent attempts to reconcile the two.[1] Nevertheless, *Civilization and Its Discontents*, appearing three years after *Freudianism*, elaborated statements dating from the beginning of Freud's career on the role of sexual repression in the formation of civilization, a line of thought that Vološinov, unlike recent Marxist thinkers, did not take up.[2] And Vološinov's preoccupation with Nietzsche and Schopenhauer, critical figures in their own right, seems myopic in the context of Freud's own writings, which were already expansive in 1927.

But beneath these two somewhat polemical strains of *Freudianism* is an insightful if limited critique of Freud as a semiotic thinker, as a theoretician of

[1] For attempts from the standpoint of psychoanalysis, see Erich Fromm, *Beyond the Chains of Illusion: My Encounter with Marx and Freud* (New York: Simon and Schuster, 1962); From the standpoint of Marxism, see Louis Althusser's extremely tentative use of the Freudian concept of overdetermination in "Contradiction and Overdetermination," in *For Marx*, trans. Ben Brewster (London: Penguin Press, 1969), pp. 87-129.

[2] Joan Riviere, trans., *The Standard Edition of the Complete Psychological Works of Sigmund Freud* (hereafter cited as *Standard Edition*), ed. James Strachey, 24 vols. (London: The Hogarth Press and The Institute of Psycho-Analysis, 1953-1974), 21 (1961): 57-145.

signs and their functions in human affairs. Vološinov argued that there were three necessary conditions of any psychology: a social focus, an objective method, and an analysis of the phenomenon of language. That Vološinov judged psychoanalysis to lack the three is far less important than the fact that he brought them to bear on it at all. His attempt constitutes a structuralist reading of psychoanalysis at a time when these terms of criticism were newly discovered and relatively unarticulated and untested.

A generation later, modern structuralists, benefiting from the intervening studies of language and culture based on the method of Saussure, would again bring these concepts to bear on Freud, this time with a richness of result that could as well have been Vološinov's.[3] The French psychiatrist Jacques Lacan caused an upheaval in the French psychoanalytic circle and motivated a broad rereading of Freud himself with the discovery that Freudian texts were structural analyses of an aspect of language, and that they anticipated some of Saussure's own first principles.[4]

Apparently, Vološinov could not see that thread of linguistic preoccupation in Freud, perhaps for lack of a power of perception that only the movement of intellectual history could awaken. And yet this failure of reading is not to Vološinov's discredit unless it is to the discredit of Freud himself, for there is no evidence that Freud self-consciously identified his treatment of language as even a secondary aspect of his work.

There are excuses for Freud's failure to see his own linguistic bent: his preoccupation with administering a new therapeutic establishment and his polemical defense of the theory of sexuality against the revisions of his own students and the outrage of laypersons. Nonetheless, language is not discussed in

---

[3] Ferdinand de Saussure, *Course in General Linguistics*, trans. Wade Baskin (New York: McGraw-Hill, 1959). For a selection of current structuralist views, see Jacques Ehrmann, ed., *Structuralism* (Garden City, N. Y.: Anchor Books, 1970); and Michael Lane, comp., *Introduction to Structuralism* (New York: Basic Books, 1970).

[4] For an introduction to Lacan's approach, see Anthony Wilden, "Lacan and the Discourse of the Other," which appears with Wilden's translation of Lacan, "The Function of Language in Psychoanalysis," and an extensive bibliography in Anthony Wilden, tr. & ed., *The Language of the Self* (Baltimore: Johns Hopkins Press, 1968). See also Jan Miel, "Jacques Lacan and the Structure of the Unconscious," in Ehrmann, *Structuralism*, pp. 94–101. Many of Lacan's essays appear in *Ecrits* (Paris: Éditions du Seuil, 1966). In addition to "The Function of Language in Psychoanalysis," other papers of Lacan's in English are: "Seminar on 'The Purloined Letter,' " in *French Freud: Structural Studies in Psychoanalysis*, ed. Jeffrey Mehlman, Yale French Studies 48 (New Haven: Yale University Press, 1972), pp. 39-72; Miel's translation of "The Insistence of the Letter in the Unconscious," in Ehrmann, *Structuralism*, pp. 101-137; and "Of Structure as an Inmixing of an Otherness Prerequisite to Any Subject Whatever," in *The Languages of Criticism and the Sciences of Man*, ed. Richard Macksey and Eugenio Donato (Baltimore: Johns Hopkins Press, 1970), pp. 186-200.

any of Freud's correspondence with psychoanalytic colleagues.[5] Nor does it appear in the work of any of Freud's successors, except as the early discovery by C. G. Jung of the word association test, which passed out of Jung's work after his break with Freud.[6]

Vološinov contributed to the reversal of his own judgment against Freud. He was a direct influence on Prague School structuralist research on language and culture which, through the work of Roman Jakobson, profoundly influenced the anthropology of Claude Lévi-Strauss—who in turn influenced Lacan.[7] Thus it is not strange that the discourse model with which Vološinov assessed Freud's shortcomings was essentially the same as that with which Lacan constructed the epistemology that demonstrated Freud's structural significance.

And yet Vološinov's three criteria for judgment against Freud may also be stronger than those of Lacan's generation, for in an elaborated structuralism, a valid (which is to say structural) linguistic analysis is objective and social by definition. Once the preoccupation with structure is discovered in Freud, the other two properties follow by implication.

But if the three properties are studied independently, as Vološinov studied them, Freud's handling of objectivity appears sketchy, and his treatment of the social focus, even with *Civilization and Its Discontents* taken into account, somewhat conflicted. Vološinov's criteria still constitute an effective means of access to Freud's position as a linguistic thinker—for Vološinov and for modern structuralism as well.

A Theory of Language

For Vološinov, language comprises the content and data of the psyche and as such is saturated with the social values of the user's speech community. As

---

[5] Sigmund Freud *et al.*, *Letters*, comp. and ed. Ernst L. Freud, trans. Tania Stern and James Stern (New York: Basic Books, 1960); Sigmund Freud and Karl Abraham, *A Psycho-Analytic Dialogue: Sigmund Freud and Karl Abraham, 1907-26*, ed. Hilda C. Abraham and Ernst L. Freud, trans. Bernard Marsh and Hilda C. Abraham (New York: Basic Books, 1965); Sigmund Freud and C. G. Jung, *The Freud-Jung Letters: The Correspondence between Sigmund Freud and C. G. Jung*, ed. William McGuire, Trans. Ralph Manheim and R. F. C. Hull, Bollingen Series 94 (Princeton: Princeton University Press, 1974); and Sigmund Freud and Arnold Zweig, *The Letters of Sigmund Freud and Arnold Zweig*, ed. Ernst L. Freud, trans. Elaine Robson-Scott and William Robson-Scott (New York: Harcourt Brace Jovanovich, 1970).

[6] C. G. Jung, "The Association Method," *American Journal of Psychology* 21 (1910): 219-269.

[7] See Anthony Wilden, "The Symbolic, the Imaginary and the Real: Lacan, Lévi-Strauss, and Freud," and "Metaphor and Metonymy: Freud's Semiotic Model of Condensation and Displacement," in *System and Structure: Essays in Communication and Exchange* (London: Tavistock Publications, 1972), pp. 1-30, 31-62.

"outward speech," it has the ideological function of justifying actions to others; as "inner speech," the constant internal monologue that for Vološinov comprises consciousness, it has an analogous function of self-justification.

Vološinov believed that Freud lacked a theory of language, that instead of analyzing his essentially verbal data, Freud accepted them naively, and built from them a structure of a fictitious individual psyche of which they were to be the product. Lacking such a critical theory of language, Freud allegedly failed to recognize the ideological nature of the verbal data of psychoanalysis, taking them instead to be an objective reflection of psychical reality. Freud's chief fiction for Vološinov was "the unconscious."

For example, Vološinov stated:

> Freud's whole psychological construct is based fundamentally on human verbal utterances; it is nothing but a special kind of interpretation of utterances. All these utterances are, of course, constructed in the *conscious sphere of the psyche*. To be sure, Freud distrusts the surface motives of consciousness; he tries, instead, to penetrate to deeper levels of the psychical realm. Nevertheless, Freud does not take utterances in their objective aspect, does not seek out their physiological or social roots; instead he attempts to find the true motives of behavior in the utterances themselves—the patient is himself supposed to provide him information about the depths of the "unconscious." [p. 76].

Vološinov believes that Freud "takes the patient's word for it" that he lacks an objective mode of analyzing the language he encounters. The lack of such a theory arises as an issue even before the issue of objectivity ("take utterances in their objective aspect") or of a social focus ("seeks out their . . . social roots").

In fact, whether or not Vološinov would have approved of it, such a theory exists in Freud's earliest and most important work. It has a specific locus, the concepts of "condensation" and "displacement," the two structural modes of dream construction discussed at length in *The Interpretation of Dreams* (1900).[8] Indeed, they may be the fundamental concepts of psychoanalysis.

In his lengthy presentation of psychoanalytic theory, Vološinov very explicitly discusses those concepts that pertain to the psychical construct he finds so invalid: the unconscious, free association, the Oedipus complex, censorship, resistance, and others. Yet in his discussion of dream formation, the concepts of condensation and displacement notably lack the type of foregrounding that others receive in his argumentation [p. 51]. At best, the two are submerged within the general discussion, indistinguishable from their many superficial and theoretically secondary manifestations. At worst, Vološinov may not have recognized the significance of the two concepts at all.

[8] Trans. James Strachey, in *Standard Edition*, vols. 4 and 5 (1953), especially pp. 134-509.

As Freud stated it, condensation and displacement are the two means by which wishes otherwise unacceptable to a person can gain a degree of distortion and camouflage that allows them to be partially expressed. In condensation, one or more elements of the underlying wish ("latent dream thought") are represented by one of their parts or properties, which serves as its "condensed substitute." Thus in the dream itself ("manifest dream content") a person might be condensed into one of his possessions or a phrase that he or she utters; two or more different persons might be represented by a single individual with a property common to them all, such as sex, age, or a feature of physiognomy. In the manifest dream itself, the condensation represents the full element of the underlying wish.

In displacement, an element of the underlying wish was represented by some other thing to which—at least for the dreamer—it bore a resemblance, for example, as in one of Freud's patient's dreams, when climbing down the stairs represented engaging in sexual intercourse with a person of a lower socioeconomic class.[9]

There are, of course an infinite number of possible relations of wholes to parts and of things to similar things, which means a virtually unlimited variety of subtypes of condensation and displacement. Freud explored the taxonomy of such subtypes in some detail (for example, a thing displaced by another thing through a pun on its name or a thing condensed into its opposite), but he insisted that even the most bizarre manifestations were ultimately analyzable into condensation or displacement. The fundamental nature of condensation and displacement was confirmed as Freud extended the dream analysis to the larger semiotic realm, including pathological symptoms, "psychopathologies of everyday life" such as slips of the tongue and jokes, and myths, religious rituals, and works of verbal and plastic art. The importance of the two concepts is defined by the extent of the phenomena they analyze. By a truly structural reading of Freud, all of the notional, nonstructural, psychologized concepts that Vološinov condemns—the unconscious, the Oedipus concept, censorship, and the rest—are subordinate to condensation and displacement, merely names for generalizations or commentaries on the results of structural analyses of such psychoanalytic phenomena as dreams, symptoms, and free associations.

Yet the two concepts do not emerge in their authority and simplicity as Vološinov discusses *The Interpretation of Dreams*:

> The laws for the formation of the symbols that replace the objects of a repressed impulse are very complex. Their governing aim comes down to a matter of maintaining some, even if only remote, *connection* with the repressed presentation, on the one hand, and, on the other, of assuming a shape that would be wholly *legal*, correct,

[9] *Interpretation*, pp. 238-240.

and acceptable for the conscious. This is accomplished by merging several images into one composite image, by interpolating a series of intermediary images linked both with the repressed presentation and with the one present in the manifest content of the dream, by implementing images of exactly opposite meaning, by transferring emotions and affects from their actual objects to other, indifferent details of the dream, by turning affects into their opposites, and the like [p. 51].

The significance and simplicity of the two concepts, as well as their fundamentally linguistic nature did not escape Roman Jakobson, who recognized that Freud's condensation and displacement were equivalent to the syntagmatic and paradigmatic axes of language, the poles of combination and selection—and equivalent as well to metonymy and metaphor in poetics and contiguity and similarity disorders in aphasia.[10] In fact, the two terms are discussed by Jakobson in the context of aphasia, the same psycholinguistic disorder that, as will be shown, was the starting point for Freud's own first work in psychoanalysis.

Jakobson's equation of the two Freudian principles with those of his own linguistics constitutes the most fundamental claim for Freud as a structuralist, for syntagm and paradigm are as much as any others the maximally simple principles on which the modern science of language is founded. A science, as Albert Einstein explained for physics, seeks to explain all phenomena within its domain by rational deduction from as few basic concepts as possible:

> These fundamental concepts and postulates, which cannot be further reduced logically, form the essential part of a theory, which reason cannot touch. It is the grand object of all theory to make these irreducible elements as simple and as few in number as possible, without having to renounce the adequate representation of any empirical content whatever.[11]

By Einstein's position, and given Jakobson's own work in such areas as the theory of distinctive features in phonology,[12] it is conceivable that the task of structural linguistics has been nothing other than the explanation of language phenomena by deduction from the concepts of syntagm and paradigm. As a structuralist, Freud undertook this same task for the limited domain of psychoanalytic symptoms, a subset of significative phenomena. Vološinov is not incorrect in stating that *The Interpretation of Dreams* shows Freud analyzing a

---

[10] See "Two Aspects of Language and Two Types of Aphasic Disturbance," Roman Jakobson and Morris Halle, *Fundamentals of Language*, Part II, Janua Linguarum Series Minor 1 (The Hague: Mouton, 1957), pp. 80-82.

[11] "On the Method of Theoretical Physics," in *Ideas and Opinions*, trans. Sonja Barmann (New York: Crown, 1954), p. 272.

[12] See the essays in Roman Jakobson, *Selected Writings* vol. 1 (The Hague: Mouton, 1962).

countless variety of symbol forms: things condensed onto words, word sounds displaced onto other word sounds, causes condensed onto effects, entities displaced onto their opposites, or, as a passage to be cited in another context [p. 127] will show, some of Freud's own favorites: "assonance, verbal ambiguity, temporal ambiguity, temporal coincidence without connection in meaning."

In the context of Vološinov's failure to recognize this strand of Freud, the achievement of the recent structuralists seems to have been that of allowing Freud's analysis of language to emerge in its own right against precisely such concepts as the unconscious, which Vološinov correctly believed to have given Freudianism its acclaim and notoriety. For example, Lacan states:

> Take up the work of Freud ... at the *Traumdeutung* to remind yourself that the dream has the structure of a sentence or, rather, to stick to the letter of the work, of a rebus; that is to say, it has the structure of a form of writing, of which the child's dream represents the primordial ideography and which, in the adult, reproduces the simultaneously phonetic and symbolic use of signifying elements, which can also be found in the hieroglyphs of ancient Egypt and in the characters still used in China.[13]

The differences between Vološinov's and Lacan's comments reveal their differences in perception even when they are not in mutual contradiction. Language—or Freud's insensitivity to language—is discussed on one of four pages of *Freudianism*; Lacan claims that language can be found to be discussed on every other page of Freud's own complete works. Vološinov wrote, "The unconscious is nonverbal, it abhors words" [p. 37]; Lacan states, in a slogan that might be an anthem of French structuralism, "the unconscious is structured like a language."

It is undoubtedly a radical reading of any thinker as expansive as Freud to claim that the last 38 years of his work, years filled with major conceptual revision and major studies, were basically an elaboration of two concepts, indeed of concepts of linguistics, that occurred in a single work written within the first 10 years of his career. But nonetheless it is reading with some support. Vološinov himself stated that the method of *The Interpretation of Dreams* "became classical and standard procedures for psychoanalysis as a whole [p. 50]" that it constituted Freud's "most substantive research [p. 50]." Freud himself thought no less of it, although neither he nor Vološinov mentioned its linguistic importance. In a letter written the year of the publication of *The Interpretation of Dreams* to Freud's colleague Wilhelm Fleiss, Freud stated that he felt it to be his most important work.[14] Within the text itself he called it "the royal road to a knowledge of the unconscious," and in a sixth edition published three years after *Freudianism*, he had not changed his feelings:

[13] "The Function of Language in Psychoanalysis," p. 30.
[14] 12 June 1900, *Letters*, p. 240.

> It contains, even according to my present-day judgement, the most valuable of all the discoveries it has been my good fortune to make. Insight such as this falls to one's lot but once in a lifetime.[15]

James Strachey's monumental work of assemblage, textual editing, and bibliography, the 24-volume *Standard Edition of the Complete Psychological Works of Sigmund Freud*, has, since 1953 when its first volume appeared, provided readers with grounds for an appraisal of Freud that were without equal for Vološinov or any earlier critic. Although Vološinov cited major works, such as the *Interpretation*, *Studies on Hysteria*, and *Beyond the Pleasure Principle*, the nature of his reading may be determined to some extent by the inavailability of texts. Nonethless, Vološinov offers a critical history of Freudian thought, and it is perhaps here that his position regarding linguistic analysis in Freud is most evident.

For example, Vološinov placed *The Interpretation of Dreams* in the second, "classical" period of Freud's work, a period whose style was allegedly "dry and businesslike [p. 30]" and whose conception of the unconscious "bore an emphatically positivistic character [p. 30]." (In light of Vološinov's endorsement at the opening of *Freudianism* of objective, positivistic psychological method, his attribution to these properties to *The Interpretation of Dreams* must be seen as praise.) But it is the conceptualization of the unconscious that is the theme through which Vološinov categorizes his chronology, his first period dominated not by *The Interpretation of Dreams* but by the Freud-Breuer *Studies on Hysteria* of 1893-1895.[16]

In fact, Freud's first psychoanalytic statements were earlier yet, in *On Aphasia* (1891), statements about language rather than about the unconscious. Previously Freud has evident success in the conventional neurological investigation of the nervous system of eels (1877) and a discovery and application of cocaine as an anaesthetic (1884).[17] *On Aphasia*, however, contains the keystone revelation of the young neurologist, that verbal slips and "mistakes" virtually identical to those made routinely by the brain-damaged could be found in the speech of healthy persons.[18] These verbal errors were "psychopathologies of everyday life," the objective data that in the first great

---

[15] *Interpretation*, p. 608; and "Preface to the Third (Revised English) Edition" (1931), p. xxxii.

[16] Sigmund Freud and Josef Breuer, *Studies on Hysteria*, trans. Alix Strachey and James Strachey, in *Standard Edition*, vol. 2 (1955).

[17] See Ernest Jones, *The Life and Works of Sigmund Freud*, vol. 1: *1856-1900: The Formative Years and the Great Discoveries* (New York: Basic Books, 1953), especially pp. 38, 72, 78-98.

[18] Trans. E. Stengel (New York: International Universities Press, 1953).

years of Freud's work would constitute, after dreams, the basis for psychoanalytic investigation.

In *On Aphasia* is dramatized the domination of Freud's thought by the physicalistic paradigms of his medical education and the emergence of a new concern. In his thoroughly neurological monograph, the young Freud went so far as to supply a theory of language.[19] "Word-presentations" were claimed to be linked in the mind by "association" to "object-associations." A normal person's acquisition of speech, spelling, reading, and writing was explained as developments of associative channels from the mental "images" of word-presentations to the specific organs of the body that effect them in behavior, a statement congenial with Vološinov's "physiological processes in the nervous system and in the organs of speech and perception," one of his three components of verbal reactions [p. 21]. Aphasia itself was postulated to be a disturbance of either the images comprising the word-presentations or the associational links between them and the object-associations.

A structuralist might see here a pre-Saussurean conception of "the diacritical nature of the sign," a fundamental principle of structural linguistics. If it is such a conception, it is nonetheless far more referential than anything Saussure intended, more materialistic than conventional in its epistemology.[20] The process of "association" in Freud's model could have derived from the faculty psychology and associationalist epistemology of the nineteenth century. Indeed Freud had won a prize as a youth for his translation of the works of John Stuart Mill.[21] Such a borrowing from associationalism puts into perspective Vološinov's criticism of the influence on Freud of Romantic philosophers.

In addition to his general charge that Freud lacked a theory of language, Vološinov criticizes Freud for "turning his back on physiology from the very start [p. 34]." Given Vološinov's endorsement of the methods of behavioral psychology, this amounts to charging Freud with a lack of objectivity, the second criterion, to be discussed later. And yet, the theoretical metaphors of the physical sciences and their adjacent philosophies provided Freud with the only models he had for the new data he was discovering. In the absence of a structural tradition, physicalistic models were for Freud, as for Vološinov, the model of scientific explanation. For example, "amalgamation" and "distortion," preliminary versions of condensation and displacement, were discussed in an 1897 letter to Wilhelm Fleiss in an analogy to chemistry:

Phantasies are constructed by a process of amalgamation and distortion analogous to the decomposition of a chemical body which is compounded with another one. For

[19] Ibid., pp. 72-78.
[20] *Course*, pp. 65-70.
[21] Jones, *Freud*, vol. 1, pp. 55-56.

the first sort of distortion consists in a falsification of memory by a process of fragmentation in which chronological relations in particular are neglected. . . . A fragment of the visual scene is joined up with a fragment of the auditory one and made into a phantasy, while the fragment left over is linked up with something else.[22]

In "The Unconscious" (1915), Freud redeveloped the associationalist model of *On Aphasia*, this time as a metapsychology for psychoanalysis. His concepts of the psychical systems, the energy discharge mechanisms of cathexis, and other constructs developed by then in his psychoanalytic work took the place of aphasia as the focus for explanation.[23]

Only in the late essay, "Inhibitions, Symptoms and Anxiety" (1926), does Freud recognize that fully semiotic models have come to displace those of the physical sciences in his elucidation of psychical phenomena. As he stated regarding the psychoanalytically-central matter of anxiety:

> whereas I formerly believed that anxiety *invariably arose automatically by an economic process*, my present conception of anxiety as a *signal given* [my italics] by the ego in order to affect the pleasure-unpleasure agency does away with the necessity of considering the economic factor.[24]

In his first attempt to map the terrain of what would become psychoanalysis, "Project for a Scientific Psychology" (1894), Freud used a standard model of brain functioning as a heuristic. The plan was ambitious, given the uncertainty of theory and data at the time, but it was also dominated by the thinking of a conventional physician. When Freud had finally succeeded in visualizing the new phenomena of psychoanalysis outside the grids of his training, it was in the sophisticated structural models of language.

No reformulation of physical models in the context of language has been more important to Freudianism than the movement from the mechanistic "association" of *On Aphasia* to "free association," a device that would persist to the end of Freud's career as the crux of his therapeutic method. "Association" was taken out of the brain and placed in the interaction between patient and therapist. A psychoanalytic patient was ordered to utter whatever came to mind during his therapy session, to "free associate" from one utterance to the next.[25] By so doing, Freud postulated, the patient would bring to full consciousness the underlying messages that the patient's symptoms only covertly expressed.

[22] Letter to Wilhelm Fleiss, 22 December 1897, in "Extracts from the Fleiss Papers," trans. Eric Mosbacher and James Strachey, in *Standard Edition* 1 (1966): 252.

[23] Trans. C. M. Baines, in *Standard Edition* 14 (1957): 159-204.

[24] Trans. Alix Strachey, in *Standard Edition* 20 (1959): 140.

[25] See Sigmund Freud, *New Introductory Lectures on Psycho-Analysis*, trans. James Strachey," in *Standard Edition* 22 (1964), especially pp. 10-14, 48-54.

For Freud, free association constituted an orderly linguistic analysis of the route from an underlying, repressed content to its distorted superficial manifestation. This is much like what transformational grammarians 50 years later would call the recovery of deletions between deep and surface structures.[26]

Freud himself made the connection between "association" and "free association" as early as *The Interpretation of Dreams*:

> It may be that free play of ideas with a fortuitous chain of associations is to be found in destructive organic processes; what is regarded as such in the psychoneuroses can always be explained as an effect of the censorship's influence upon a train of thought which has been pushed into the foreground by purposive ideas that have remained hidden. It has been regarded as an unfailing sign of an association being uninfluenced by purposive ideas if the associations (or images) in question seem to be interrelated in what is described as a "superficial" manner—by assonance, verbal ambiguity, temporal coincidence without connection in meaning, or by any association of the kind that we allow In Jokes or in play upon words. This characteristic is present in chains of thought which lead from the elements of a dream to the intermediate thoughts and from these to the dream-thoughts proper; we have seen instances of this—not without astonishment—in many dream analyses. No connection was too loose, no joke too bad, to serve as a bridge from one thought to another. But the true explanation of this easy-going state of things is soon found. *Whenever one psychical element is linked with another by an objectionable or superficial association, there is also a legitimate and deeper link between them which is subjected to the resistance of the censorship* [Freud's italics].[27]

Free association was precisely the means of retracing the paths of condensation and displacement, of establishing deductive links between underlying messages and superficial symptoms. It also verified that condensation and displacement could not be further reduced, in Einstein's sense, to a more primitive single concept, through the fact that the analyst could not determine a priori—without free association—whether a given symbol-formation was the result of the one process or the other.

Thus, for example, Freud's own conjecture on the meaning of a symptom as a condensation was proven incorrect by the free associations of one of his most famous patients, "Little Hans." Freud had guessed that a butterfly in one of the child's dreams symbolized a woman, through the condensation of the pattern of its wings from that of the woman's dress. The child's associations indicated, instead, that the slow movement of the insect's wings was a displacement from the movement of a woman's legs.[28] That Freud happened to be correct about

[26] See Noam Chomsky, *Aspects of a Theory of Syntax* (Cambridge, Mass.: MIT Press, 1965), especially pp. 128-147.

[27] *Interpretation*, pp. 529-530.

[28] *From the History of an Infantile Neurosis*, trans. Alix Strachey and James Strachey, in *Standard Edition* 17 (1955): 90.

the meaning of the symbol was semiotically less important than his inability to second-guess the results of free association.

The crucial presupposition behind "condensation" and "displacement" and the use of free association as a therapeutic tool was that dreams, hysterical symptoms, and the other forms of unconscious expression were *meaningful*. In Saussurean terms, these phenomena were "signifiers" that corresponded to "signifieds." Articulated in *The Interpretation of Dreams*, the idea appeared a decade before Saussure's courses. Yet, if this attribution of meaning to symptoms is the driving force of *The Interpretation of Dreams*, it had already been stated explicitly three years before in the basic therapeutic premise of the *Studies on Hysteria*. For the *Studies on Hysteria* reported that physical maladies that previously had been approached unsuccessfully as purely somatic disorders were shown to be symbolizations—to be *meaningful*—covert expressions of messages. Example after example in the *Studies on Hysteria* involves the revelation under hypnosis (Freud had not yet developed free association and was still using the method of Charcot, which gave only temporary relief from the large-scale pattern of symptom formation) that a particular physical disorder was a pun, a bodily statement of some idea that the patient could not declare explicitly.

For Frau Cäcilie M., hypnosis disclosed that violent pains in the right heel expressed fears of being unable to " 'find herself on a right footing' " (" 'finden das richtige oder rechte Auftreten' ") with friends of her husband's to whom she had been introduced.[29] If Vološinov is entitled in any way to allow the *Studies on Hysteria* to dominate his chronology of Freud's thought, it is on the basis of such decoding, of the discovery of a dimension of signification, indeed, as Lacan would say, of a Language. What were regarded as merely physical, nonrational processes would henceforth be seen as signs.

Thus it was the discovery of the significative nature of such symptoms that distinguished psychoanalysis from traditional, physicalistic medicine. But, the hypothesis that a deep "inner" meaning could be hidden in such a symptom or in a dream or slip of the tongue was at the same time the royal road to the exploitation of psychoanalysis: its vulgarization, sham appeal, sensationalism, and vulnerability to petty mysticism. Freud himself weakened the linguistic respectability of his theory by vacillating later in his career on the hypothesis of a fixed sexual symbolism, a set of nonlinguistic, motivated signs as opposed to the arbitrary conventionalized signs of language.[30] Especially with such a fixed

---

[29] "On the Mechanism of Hysterical Phenomena," trans. James Strachey, in *Standard Edition* 3 (1962): 34; "Über den psychischen Mechanismus hysterischer phänomene," in *Sigmund Freud: Studienausgabe*, ed. James Strachey, 10 vols. (Frankfurt: S. Fischer Verlag, 1970-1975), 1:19.

[30] See *Five Lectures on Psycho-Analysis*, trans. James Strachey, in *Standard Edition* 11 (1955): 36.

symbolism, by which any long, thin object could symbolize a penis, it became possible for any person to place a "Freudian interpretation" on any utterance or behavior. Without a rigorous underpinning in condensation and displacement, psychoanalysis might as well have been a form of sophistry. Thus, Vološinov aptly railed against the excesses of a popular Freudianism, but instead of focusing on its depiction of humans as sexual animals outside of history and society, he might with equal justification have attacked the Freudian thesis of the meaningfulness of symptoms, at once the essence and greatest liability of Freudianism.

Objective Method

It was not enough for Vološinov that a psychology have a theory of language. That theory must also be objective (and have, as a later section will discuss, a social base). Just as Vološinov did not feel that Freud's use of "verbal reactions" amounted to a theory of language, he did not feel that the approach was objective:

> Psychology must implement *objective methods* and study the *materially expressed behavior of human beings* in the conditions of the natural and *social* environment [Vološinov's italics]. Such are the requirements Marxism makes incumbent upon psychology [p. 22].

Vološinov had given a linguistic definition to the "content of the psyche" through his concept of "inner speech." Speech in the ordinary sense—discourse, as he frequently calls it—constituted a social "scenario" for human actions, their ideological justification. Thought was merely an externalization of discourse—a discourse to the self—and as such was fully in the domain of the verbal. Thus a study of the content of the psyche should operate as an objective study of language:

> The complex apparatus of verbal reactions functions in all its fundamental aspects also when the subject says nothing about his experiences but only undergoes them "in himself," since, if he is conscious of them, a process of *inner* ("covert") speech occurs (we do, after all, think and feel and desire with the help of words; without inner speech we could not become conscious of anything in ourselves). This process of inner speech is just as material as is outward speech.
>
> And so, if, in a psychological experiment, we replace the subject's "inner experience" with its *verbal equivalent* (inner and outward speech or only inner speech), we still can maintain the integrity and continuity of external, material apprehension. That is how a psychological experiment is viewed by the objectivists [p. 21].

The study of language for Vološinov had two material components and one semantic component, the studies of:

1. *The physical sound of articulated words;*
2. *Physiological processes in the nervous system and in the organs of speech and perception;*
3. *A special set of features and processes that correspond to the "meaning" of a verbal statement and the "understanding" of that meaning by another person. . . .* The formation of verbal meanings requires the establishment of connections among visual, motor, and auditory reactions over the course of long and organized social intercourse between individuals. However, this set, too, is completely objective inasmuch as all the ways and means that serve the formation of verbal connections fall within external apprehension and are on principle accessible to objective methods of study, even if those methods are not purely physiological ones [p. 21].

Vološinov's strong if qualified endorsement of behaviorist—objective, materialist—psychology is reflected in the predominance of physical study in his listing: acoustical phonetics, neurolinguistics, and articulatory phonetics, and even in the formation of meaning falling "within external apprehension." What remains is a purely social semantics which, although it is unelaborated, seems to be an aspect of the study of ideology:

We shall never reach the real, substantive roots of any given single utterance if we look for them within the confines of the single individual organism. . . . *self-consciousness*, in the final analysis, always leads us to *class consciousness*, the reflection and specification of which it is in all its fundamental and essential respects. Here we have the *objective roots* of even the most personal and intimate verbal reactions.

How do we reach those roots?

With the help of those objective-sociological methods that Marxism has worked out for the analysis of various ideological systems—law, morality, science, world-outlook, art, religion [pp. 86–87].

Lacan, it must be noted, is diametrically opposed to Vološinov on the issue of the appropriateness of the "objective" behavioristic approach (both cite Pavlov as an example) for psychoanalysis. Indeed, the "return to Freud" itself was begun by Lacan to reverse the overwhelming revision of psychoanalysis by such reductive approaches as ego psychology, Gestalt psychology, "the analysis of defenses," and, especially, the many varieties of objectivism. The bitterness of Lacan's statement at the end of a critical analysis of an application of conditioning experiments to psychoanalysis can serve as an index of the extent of his opposition:

This monument of naïveté, in any case of a kind common enough in these matters, would not be worth so much attention if it were not the achievement of a psychoanalyst, or rather of someone who fits into his work as if by accident everything produced by a certain tendency in psychoanalysis—in the name of the theory of the ego or of the technique of the analysis of defenses—everything, that is, which is the most contrary to the Freudian experience. In this way the coherence of a sound conception of Language alone with the maintenance of this conception is revealed *a contrario*. For Freud's discovery was that of the domain of the incidence in the nature of man of his relations to the Symbolic order and the tracing of their sense right back to the most radical instances of symbolization in being. To misconstrue this Symbolic order is to condemn the discovery to oblivion, and the experience to ruin.[31]

Nonetheless, Vološinov's accusation is that psychoanalysis naively accepts personal ideology as analytic truth. "In the whole Freudian construct of a psychical conflict," Vološinov writes, "together with all the mechanisms through which it operates, we hear only the biased voice of the subjective consciousness interpreting human behavior" [p. 77]. Even if there are problems in Vološinov's concept of "objective method," his accusation warrants reply.

For his own part, Freud had been aware of the danger of subjectivity as early as the *Studies on Hysteria*. For him, the danger was that of the analyst imposing his own, subjective reading on the material, rather than being taken in by the subjectivity of the patient. Nonetheless, his statement of the problem is as direct as Vološinov's:

> I have not always been a psychotherapist. Like other neuropathologists, I was trained to employ local diagnoses and electro-prognosis, and it still strikes me myself as strange that the case histories I write should read like short stories and that, as one might say, they lack the serious stamp of science. I must console myself with the reflection that the nature of this subject is evidently responsible for this, rather than any preference of my own.[32]

In fact, Freud had a claim to an objective method: the formal nature of his work, which he distinguished from the superficial meanings of his data. If form—structure—is not itself the material or social property of Vološinov's objective method, it may nonetheless be the most important characteristic of an objective approach. And if Freud and Vološinov do not precisely agree on what constitutes such a guarantor of scientific objectivity, they do agree on what it prevents: the acceptance by the analyst of "the biased voice of the subjective consciousness."

Freud did not explicitly discuss his use of the formal method as often as one might like. Lacan would claim that it is evident everywhere in his works—except, of course, that it was not evident to Vološinov. Nonetheless, where the formal method is mentioned, it is in opposition to the interpretation of superficial meaning, as, for example, in *The Interpretation of Dreams*:

---

[31] "The Function of Language in Psycho-Analysis," pp. 37-38.
[32] *Studies on Hysteria*, p. 160.

If we wish to pursue our study of the relations between dream-content and dream-thoughts further, the best plan will be to take dreams themselves as our points of departure and consider what certain *formal* [Freud's italics] characteristics of the method of representation in dreams signify in relation to the thoughts underlying them.[33]

Similarly, in *Jokes and Their Relation to the Unconscious* (1905), it was elements of structure rather than content that were argued to qualify jokes as a phenomenon in the psychanalytic domain:

But if what makes our example a joke is not anything that resides in its thought, we must look for it in the form, in the wording in which it is expressed. We have only to study the peculiarity of its form of expression to grasp what may be termed the verbal or expressive technique of this joke, something which must stand in an intimate relation with the essence of the joke, since, if it is replaced by something else, the character and effect of the joke disappear.[34]

Likewise, the differences between poetry and mundane fantasy as expressions of the unconscious was to be located in the structure of their presentation—not in their literal meanings. Freud stated in "Creative Writers and Day-Dreaming" (1907):

The writer softens the character of his egoistic day-dreams by altering and disguising it, and he bribes us by the purely formal—that is, aesthetic—yield of pleasure which he offers us in the presentation of his phantasies.[35]

The objectivity of Freud's method can be seen in the nature of the results it yields as well as in the passages in which it is mentioned. It is here that Freud's anticipation of specific insight of structural linguistics serves him best, in validating the objectivity of his method. Freud used the analytic approaches of what would be structural linguistics to discover the nature of the wholly new order of human life he had discovered, and in fact he frequently compared the phenomenon studies by psychoanalysis to Language, a language, or a language family. The level of detail to which he pursues his comparison suggests that it was not meant as a mere figure of speech. For example:

... the unconscious speaks more than one dialect. According to the differing psychological conditions governing and distinguishing the various forms of neurosis, we find regular modifications in the way in which unconscious mental impulses are expressed. While the gesture-language of hysteria agrees on the whole with the picture-language of dreams and visions, etc., the thought-language of obsessional

---

[33] P. 329.
[34] Trans. James Strachey, in *Standard Edition* 8 (1960): 17.
[35] Trans. I. F. Grant Duff, in *Standard Edition* 9 (1959): 153.

neurosis and of the paraphrenias (dementia praecox and paranoia) exhibits special idiomatic peculiarities... For instance, what a hysteric expresses by vomiting an obsessional will express by painstaking protective measures against infection, while a paraphrenic will be led to complaints or suspicions that he is being poisoned. These are all of them different representations of the patient's wish to become pregnant which have been repressed into the unconscious, or of his defensive reaction against that wish.[36]

The discovery in condensation and displacement of what amount to the syntagm and paradigm is only the most basic of Freud's linguistic insight. Freud examined the "grammar" of the unconscious in a very literal sense. He charted the structures of conditional and consequential clauses as major structural units of dreams.[37] Patterns of logical inference were drawn to show links between symptoms acquired by one hysteric from another.[38] The use of the speaker as a point of orientation, a form of "deixis" in grammer, was found to operate in dreams that were otherwise so distorted that all other points of contact with underlying sources had been camouflaged.[39] The implicative structure of a first-person embedded sentence (e.g., "I don't ever think that ____ '") was taken as an index of truth value.[40]

Freud's most powerful evocation of a modern theory of language was his use of what 50 years later would be Chomsky's "linguistic transformation" (Freud, "Verwandlung") as the chief explanatory tool in the analysis of paranoia for one of his most important case studies, *Psycho-Analytic Notes upon an Autobiographical Account of a Case of Paranoia (Dementia Paranoides).*[41] He presented detailed, principled, sentence-by-sentence derivations of each of the four forms of paranoia from a single underlying sentence, " 'I love him.' " Each of the four were argued to represent a specific option of negation furnished by the very grammar of the underlying sentence:

Delusions of jealousy contradict the subject, delusions of persecution contradict the verb,... erotomania contradicts the objects... a fourth kind of contradiction [megalomania] ... rejects the proposition as a whole.[42]

[36] Sigmund Freud, "The Claims of Psycho-Analysis to Scientific Interest," trans. James Strachey, in *Standard Edition* 13 (1953): 177-178.

[37] New Introductory Lectures, pp. 26-27.

[38] *Interpretation*, p. 150.

[39] *Ibid.*, p. 338.

[40] "Constructions in Analysis," trans. James Strachey, in *Standard Edition* 23 (1964): 262-263.

[41] The German term appears in *'Psychoanalytische Bemerkungen über einen autobiographisch beschriebenen Fall von paranoia (Dementia paranoidea)*, in *Sigmund Freud Gessamelte Werke*, ed. Anna Freud, 18 (1946-48). (London: Imago, 1954) 8:299-302. The translation is by Allx Strachey and James Strachey, in *Standard Edition*, 12 (1958): 9-82.

[42] *Psycho-Analytic Note*, pp. 64–65.

To derive two of the varieties, Freud used a specific subject-object switching transformation that he called "projection." Triggered by an initial negative element, which changed, for example, " 'I love him' " into " 'I hate him,' " an intermediate step in the derivation of delusions of persecution, projection switched subject and object to yield "he hates me." There is no compensatory insertion here of the copula and 'by' as in the transformation of an active sentence into a passive such as "he is hated by me."[43]

Only through psychoanalytic reconstruction could a language user, including the speaker himself, determine if "I hate him" and "He hates me" on any given occasion had their explicit, mundane meanings or were instead camouflaged representations of "I love him." In the light of such Formalist concepts as the "de-automatization" of a structure and the "making strange" of a poetic device, projection is a striking means for allowing the expression of that which otherwise would go unexpressed, namely the paranoid's feelings of homosexual love.[44] The camouflaged product, the paranoid symptom, is a perfectly solipsistic poem unnoticed as such in the normal commerce of language—an object hidden in plain view.

For the transformationalists, for whom the structuralists are an intellectual source, Freud's "projection" offers insight on the major question of whether meaning is preserved among formally related sentences. The idea of an "objective content" underlying related passives, questions, cleft sentences, and other agnates arose in the earliest transformational grammars in the form of the "kernel string"; radical alteration of transformational theory since then has not done away with the basic idea.[45] Freud argued that meaning was preserved amid transformations that converted a sentence into what might seem to be its opposite, and the presupposition that made such a claim possible was that paranoia represented nothing other than a specialized use of language, corresponding to a special set of grammatical rules by which mundane usage was systematically reanalyzed. Meaning was preserved in the transformation of "I love him" into "He loves me"—in the context of paranoia.

Like such philosophers of language as Wittgenstein, Strawson, and Grice,

---

[43] See Chomsky, *Aspects*, pp. 103-106.

[44] See *Readings in Russian Poetics: Formalist and Structuralist Views*, Ladislav Matejka and Krystyna Pomorska, eds. (Cambridge, Mass.: MIT Press, 1971), especially Juri Tynjanov, "On Literary Evolution," trans. C. A. Lupow, pp. 66-78, and Roman Jakobsen, "The Dominant," trans. Herbert Eagle, pp. 82-87. For further reading on this aspect of Freud's anticipation of modern linguistics, see Neal Bruss, "The Transformation in Freud," *Semiotica*, forthcoming.

[45] See Ronald Langackre, "Movement Rules in Functional Perspective," *Language* 50 (1974): 630-664; and Barbara Hall Partee, "On the Requirement That Transformations Preserve Meaning," in *Studies in Linguistic Semantics*, ed. Charles J. Fillmore and D. Terence Langendoen (New York: Holt, Rinehart, and Winston, 1971), pp. 1-21.

Freud defined meaning as a function of intention.[46] Like a modern information theorist, he argues that what amounts to the information value of an individual dream symbol varied directly with its specificity.[47]

If Freudianism is allowed to extend beyond the works of Freud, as it did for Vološinov, its use of formal method can be discovered in the word association test developed by Freud's protege C. G. Jung early in his career. The association method was explicitly structural and important enough to both Freud and Jung to be the subject of Jung's address at Clark University in 1910 when they came to America for the first time.[48] The test provided the rudiments of a "logico-linguistic" analysis of words uttered by patients freely associating on individual words presented by the therapist. The structural category of a patient's response—not its meaning, as in revisions of Jung's theory—was taken as an index of psychological character type. Jung dealt with such categories as coordination, subordination, supraordination, contrast, predication expressing personal judgment, simple predication, relation of verb to subject or complement, designation of time, word structure, and phonological association. One of the most telling indices of the importance of structure for Freud was that the word association test, with its analytic detail, was abandoned as a theoretical concern by Jung upon his break with Freud.

The investigation of structure went so far that it led, in Freud's own work, to what would seem to be a totally uncharacteristic conclusion on the phenomenology of language, that consciousness was not a property of an utterance but only a variable concomitant of it.[49] Freud realized early that users of language often had no consciousness of that which was expressed by or to them, that indeed a defining property of the psychoanalytic domain was that utterances within it were sent and received without the recognition of their meanings. A paranoid would not admit in conditions other than an effective psychoanalysis (in which case he would no longer be a paranoid) that his "He hates me" meant, rather, "I love him."

For Vološinov, Freud's unexpected belief that meaning in psychoanalysis was *not* to be found in consciousness but rather in structure would be particularly appealing—but not without a social definition of structure. For Vološinov,

[46] Ludwig Wittgenstein, *Philosophical Investigations*, trans. G. E. M. Anscombe (Oxford: Blackwell, 1967); Peter Strawson, "On Referring," in *Mind*, new series 59 (1950): 320-344; and H. P. Grice, "Utterer's Meaning and Intentions," in *Philosophical Review* 78 (1969): 147-177. The Freudian locus is the *Introductory Lectures on Psycho-Analysis* (1916), trans. James Strachey, in *Standard Edition* 15 (1963): 40, 60-61.

[47] John Lyons, *Introduction to Theoretical Linguistics* (New York: Cambridge University Press, 1968), pp. 81-98; *Interpretation*, p. 340.

[48] Jung, "The Association Method."

[49] "Some Elementary Lessons in Psycho-Analysis," trans. James Strachey, in *Standard Edition* 23 (1964): 285-286.

insistence on objectivity is qualified by "the danger of falling into a naïve, mechanistic materialism" [p. 23]. Since Freud uses structure to discover meaning, there must be a theory of society standing behind his theory of structure because, for Vološinov, meanings derive from the social world:

> Language and its forms are the product of prolonged social intercourse among members of a given speech community. An utterance finds language basically already prepared for use. It is the material for the utterance and it sets constraints on the utterance's possibilities. What is characteristic of a given utterance specifically—its selection of particular words, particular kind of sentence structure, particular kind of intonation—all this is the expression of the interrelationship between speakers and of the whole complex set of social circumstances under which the exchange of words takes place [p. 79].

Social Context

Vološinov's criterion that psychoanalysis have a social focus is one on which the other two criteria are dependent; a theory of language and methodological objectivity are ineffective unless the enterprise in which they operate is recognized as social. So pervasive is Vološinov's insistence on social focus that the other two criteria are never discussed in isolation from it. His position is particularly uncompromising:

> *The verbal component of behavior is determined in all the fundamentals and essentials of its content by objective-social factors.*
> The social environment is what has given a person words and what has joined words with specific meanings and value judgments; the same social environment continues incessantly to determine and control a person's verbal reactions throughout his entire life.
> Therefore, nothing verbal in human behavior (inner and outward speech equally) can under any circumstances be reckoned to the account of the individual subject in isolation; the verbal is not his property but the property of his *social group* (his social milieu) [p. 86].

Social focus arises as a concern of Freud and his affirmation by Lacan in three forms: as an epistemological property of language itself, in the psychoanalytic conception of society, and in the particularly social aspect of the actual psychoanalytic interaction between patient and analyst.

Vološinov tends to claim that Freud is thoroughly individualistic. Of the three criteria, the matter of social focus is least discussed in the Freudian texts. Nonetheless, it remains to be determined whether or not Freud was as lacking in social theory in each of its three respects as Vološinov claimed—a prior question to whether anything Freud offered was valid.

Language as a Social Phenomenon

Freud fell into a dichotomy between individual and social phenomena in psychoanalysis, a paradoxical and problematic conceptualization from which psychoanalysis has yet fully to recover. In *Group Psychology and the Analysis of the Ego* (1921) he distinguished between the "social phenomena" of the transference neuroses, such as "the relations of an individual to his parents and to his brothers and sisters, to the object of his love, and to his physician," and individual, " 'narcissistic' processes . . . in which the satisfaction of his instincts is partially or totally withdrawn from the influence of other people."[50] As Vološinov would have expected, the locus of the difficulty in this dichotomy was in explaining the second, individual type.

Freud himself was sufficiently aware of the social context of language use to realize the paradoxical nature of a body of symbolic structures whose articulation was for no audience. Freud could not have even claimed with such a dichotomy that the narcissistic phenomena were made by the subject for his own reception, because in their distorted expression they excluded even the subject's comprehension. Dreams, the cardinal data of psychoanalysis, were singularly opaque before free association. Freud lacked Vološinov's belief that autistic uses of language were variations on its essentially social nature, but his discussion of dreams illustrates his awareness of the difficulty in trying to make a claim for meaningfulness of utterances without audiences:

> Let us suppose, then, that someone—a patient in analysis, for instance—tells us one of his dreams. We shall assume that in this way he is making us one of the communications to which he has pledged himself by the fact of having started an analytic treatment. It is, to be sure, a communication made by inappropriate means, for dreams are not in themselves social utterances, not a means of giving information. Nor, indeed, do we understand what the dreamer was trying to say to us, and he himself is equally in the dark.[51]

The psychoanalytic concept that Vološinov most criticizes, the unconscious, can be seen as, among other things, a means of solving such a contradiction. The unconscious constitutes a domain of functioning in which the requirement that language have an audience need not hold. Psychoanalytic phenomena originate in such a solipsistic domain, not from the conscious itself. However, the problem with such a solution, as Vološinov recognizes, is that Freud is forced to claim that language does not operate in the unconscious. Such difficulties do not arise for Vološinov because with the concept of "inner speech" the idea of an

---

[50] Trans. James Strachey, in *Standard Edition* 18 (1955): 69.
[51] *New Introductory Lectures*, pp. 8-9.

audience is abstracted out of situations in which actual audiences are present and retained for those in which audiences are not.

Freud also had to face a second paradox, of seemingly asocial, acommunicative behavior revealing itself under analysis actually to be extremely pointed expressions intended for a specific audience. Without the assumption of the social nature of action, Freud faced the problem of being unable to determine in principle whether a given activity was a message or not. Thus, Freud discovered for a woman patient's act of walking down a street with her homosexual lover:

> She *wanted* [Freud's italics] her father to know occasionally of her relations with the lady, otherwise she would be deprived of the satisfaction of her keenest desire—namely revenge. So she saw to this by showing herself openly in the company of her adored one, by walking with her in the streets near her father's place of business and the like. The maladroitness, moreover, was by no means unintentional. It was remarkable, too, that both parents behaved as if they understood their daughter's secret psychology. The mother was tolerant, as though she appreciated her daughter's "retirement" as a favor to her; the father was furious, as though he realized the deliberate revenge against himself.[52]

Because Vološinov does not believe in the individual as a self-sufficient theoretical entity, he is not faced with a paradox of autistic communication. As he states in criticizing vitalistic philosophies:

> The abstract biological person, biological individual—that which has become the alpha and omega of modern ideology—does not exist at all. It is an improper abstraction. Outside society and, consequently, outside objective socioeconomic conditions, there is no such thing as a human being [p. 15].

Nor is Vološinov forced to deny the reality of those messages that exclude the comprehension even of the speaker. He admits that impulses of consciousness may conflict with each other, even attributing such inconsistency to the decline of a social class. Within "inner speech" he distinguishes between "official consciousness" and "unofficial consciousness" to capture the distinction between dominant and subversive impulses, emptying the content of the unconscious into "unofficial consciousness." Yet, because *Freudianism* does not contain reanalyses of Freudian case studies with the alternate mechanism Vološinov proposes, it is not clear whether "inner speech" and "unofficial consciousness" are anything more than terminological variants of Freud's concepts that do no more than solve the particular problem of the individual

---

[52] "The Psychogenesis of a Case of Homosexuality in a Woman," trans. Barbara Low and R. Gabler, in *Standard Edition* 18 (1957): 1-160.

category. No doubt it is a particularly vexing program: It persists in contemporary debate over whether narcissism is not actually a social phenomenon. One psychologist maintains Freud's dichotomy in distinguishing the "benignant" narcissism of self-preservation from the "malignant" form of withdrawal from reality.[53]

Yet a solution for Freud may have been found by Jacques Lacan in reversing the priority of Vološinov's inquiry, in looking at the social domain as a linguistic entity, rather than at language as a social phenomenon. Lacan returned to Freud's theory of psychical development in the light of cognitive development theory, phenomenology, and Saussurean theory of the sign, and Jakobson's analysis of pronouns and other "shifters"[54] to argue that the achievement through which the child distinguishes him- or herself out of the primal unity of infantile experience is a symbolic achievement. Lacan focuses on the "mirror stage" of childhood, in which the child, seeing his or her reflection in a mirror, first takes him- or herself as an object. This differentiation, according to Lacan, is described in Freud's theory of the differentiation of ego and superego from id, and is immediately reflected in the child's acquisition of "I," "me," and terms for "other" in language, the "shifters." The implication of the theory is that the child enters the social word when he or she is capable of making that differentiation for him- or herself and others. Psychoanalytic therapy, through this view, becomes the mode of recognition of the alienating and self-destroying forms that the construction of these identities takes for a person.

Lacan claims that the differentiation of the self as the subject of consciousness from the self as an object of consciousness—for onself and for others—as well as the recognition of others, follow the laws of language because it *is* language. As such, he declares language to be the object of study of phenomenology (the nature of consciousness and its objects) in the same way that Vološinov, through "inner speech," did for psychoanalysis. Thus in Lacan's commentary on psychoanalytic topics as the nature of neurosis, such terms as

---

[53] Edith Weigert, "Narcissism: Benignant and Malignant," in *The Courage to Love*, (New Haven: Yale University Press, 1959), pp. 119-137. See also James F. Bing, Francis McLaughlin, and Rudolf Marburg, "The Metapsychology of Narcissism," in *The Psychoanalytic Study of the Child* 14 (1959): 9-28. The issue of an individual focus in language has been raised by the Russian psychologist L. S. Vygotsky, arguing against Piaget's individualistic theory of early language development, in *Thought and Language*, ed. and trans. Eugenia Hanfmann and Gertrude Vahar (Cambridge, Mass.: MIT Press, 1962), p. 19. It also arises in the sociolinguist William Labov's critique of Chomskyan transformational grammar in "Some Principles of Linguistic Methodology," *Language and Society* 1 (1972): 97-119.

[54] Roman Jakobson, "Shifters, Verbal Categories, and the Russian Verb," *Russian Language Project* (Cambridge, Mass.: Harvard University Press, 1957). See the Wilden and Miel essays (note 4) as sources on Lacan's interpretation of Freud.

"lack" and "desire" have simultaneously phenomenological and semiotic meanings—and social meanings as well because of the social nature of language.

Yet Lacan's theory of structure goes beyond anything in Saussure, particularly in three epistemological orders—the Symbolic, the Imaginary, and the
Real—posited as simultaneous and converging domains of structure, adaptation
of structure to an objectification of the self, and of what is taken to be real. Nor
is Lacan a theoretician of the "social," which is not a phenomenon he systematically analyzes. The social world that preoccupies Vološinov is not strictly
defined by his three epistemological orders, for example. Any social thought
must be drawn from Lacan's writing, as from Freud's, and yet in a social context
Lacan's insight is valuable—that to attain a differentiated consciousness is to be
born into Language and the psychical systems elaborated by Freud. The social
world on which Vološinov bases language is already the product of a linguistic
act that Freud describes in his psychology:

> The speaking subject, if he seems to be thus a slave of language, is all the more so
> of a discourse in the universal moment of which he finds himself at birth, even if only
> by dint of his proper name.
>
> Reference to the "experience of the community" as the substance of this
> discourse settles nothing. For this experience has as its essential dimension the
> tradition which the discourse itself founds. This tradition, long before the drama of
> history gets written into it, creates the elementary structures of culture. And these
> structures reveal an ordering of possible exchanges which, even unconscious, is
> inconceivable outside the permutations authorized by language.
>
> With the results that the ethnographic duality of nature and culture is giving way to
> a ternary conception of the human condition: nature, society, and culture, the last
> term of which could well be equated to language, or that which essentially distin-
> guishes human society from natural societies.[55]

Lacan's remarks suggest that, far from standing in opposition to a theory of
society, psychoanalysis might go so far as to generate one, particularly out of its
experience with language.

Psychoanalysis and Society

The version of linguistics with which Freud was familiar, philology, may have
contributed to a psychoanalytic theory of evolution that matured into a psychoanalytic sociology. There are no indications that Freud knew of Saussure and the
synchronic focus on language that he brought, but Freud evoked in his writings
the philology, school grammar, and language pseudosciences that Saussurean
linguistics replaced. Freud was frequently taken in by their version of a protean

---

[55] "The Insistence of the Letter in the Unconscious," p. 104.

man at the dawn of language, and it may have come into his work in a naturalistic, evolutionarist point of view.

Freud was eager to recognize philological speculations that confirmed his own theses. In a pamphlet by the philologist Karl Abel, Freud found evidence that negation did not exist in "primitive" ancient languages.[56] Abel argued that basic terms of those languages often embraced wholly opposite meanings (e.g., a single word in such a language signified both "hot" and "cold"). Freud did not hesitate at the sweep of such a hypothesis, or consider that the structure of a Westerner's native language might bias such a one-directional comparison. Instead, he saw that the lack of opposite meanings corresponded with the version of displacement in which a thing was represented by its opposite. He generalized a correspondence between archaic languages and the language of unconscious expression.

By another line of thought as early as the *Studies on Hysteria* Freud tried to link the punning physical symptoms of hysterics with the language of early humans. He invoked Charles Darwin's argument in *The Expression of Emotions in Man and Animals* that figurative expressions with body references are the weak remnants of actual visceral processes from prior stages of human evolution. "Hysteria is right," Freud wrote in the *Studies on Hysteria*, "in restoring the original meaning of words in depicting its usually strong innervations."[57] The generalization was stated in *The Interpretation of Dreams*:

> Things that are symbolically connected to-day were probably united in prehistoric times by conceptual and linguistic indentity. The symbolic relation seems to be a relic and a mark of former identity.[58]

Thus at this point Freud connected language to society through a Romantic, evolutionary hypothesis: The language of primitive humans persisted in modern man as unconscious expression. But the equivalence went further: The traits that philologists such as Abel had attributed to ancient languages were also discovered by Freud in the ordinary speech of children. Thus Freud used the dreams, misunderstandings, and commonplace utterances of children as basic data; the case study of "Little Hans," despite the sketchiness of some of the material, was perhaps his most important analysis.

Freud's conclusion was that the ancient people who spoke archaic language were more childlike than modern man, that the unconscious itself constituted a

---

[56] "The Antithetical Meaning of Primal Words," trans. Alan Tyson, in *Standard Edition* 11: 155-161.

[57] Pp. 180-181.

[58] P. 352.

sanctuary for more infantile elements of the psyche. But for Freud, the concept of childhood does not betoken the Romantic myth of primal goodness untainted by civilization. Instead, it leads directly to Freud's developmental thought on the repression of impulse, the emergence of the Oedipal crisis, and the ego and the superego. At that point, what may have been a naturalistic, evolutionary mode of thought became a sociology: The movement from primitive to modern society was analogous to the development of a maturing child from infancy—and both were characterized by sexual repression. Although the concept of the unconscious was tied to the individualistic developmental model, which, as Vološinov states, had a strongly individualistic focus, it would now have a reflection in the structure of society. Society, like the mature individual, had a psychoanalytic theory of origins.

This was a late view of Freud's, expressed partially in such works as *Three Essays on the Theory of Sexuality* (1905) and *Beyond the Pleasure Principle* (1920), but also as far back as the Fleiss letters. It had its most powerful statement as *Civilization and Its Discontents*, which appeared three years after *Freudianism*. Vološinov perhaps cannot be criticized for failing to synthesize this line of thought from Freud's writings even before Freud himself. But it nonetheless fills the lack of a social thrust in the psychoanalysis which he criticized. A school of politically radical psychoanalytic thinkers developed from the hypothesis, most significantly Wilhelm Reich, Geza Roheim, and Herbert Marcuse,[59] whose *Eros and Civilization* is an attempt to reconcile Marxist theory with a version of psychoanalysis seen through *Civilization and Its Discontents*. Marcuse states:

> Sigmund Freud's proposition that civilization is based on the permanent subjugation of the human instincts has been taken for granted. His question whether the suffering thereby inflicted upon individuals has been worth the benefits of culture has not been taken too seriously—the less so since Freud himself considered the process to be inevitable and irreversible. Free gratification of man's instinctual needs is incompatible with civilized society: renunciation and delay in satisfaction are the prerequisites of progress. "Happiness," said Freud, "is no cultural value." Happiness must be subordinated to the discipline of work as full-time occupation, to the discipline of monogamic reproduction, to the established system of law and order. The methodological sacrifice of libido, its rigidly enforced deflection to socially useful activities and expressions, *is* culture.[60]

At the extreme, "polymorphous perversity," the infantile state of sensory gratification, becomes an end of revolution.[61]

---

[59] See Paul Robinson, *The Freudian Left: Wilhelm Reich, Geza Roheim, and Herbert Marcuse* (New York: Harper and Row, 1969).

[60] *Eros and Civilization* (Boston: Beacon Press, 1955), p. 1.

[61] For example, Norman O. Brown, *Love's Body* (New York: Random House, 1966), especially "Freedom," pp. 242-255.

Lacan absorbed this psychoanalytic theory of society into his concepts of the linguistic signifier and of discourse itself. Through the structural anthropology of Claude Lévi-Strauss, Lacan received Marcel Mauss's concept of "the gift" as the exchange of tokens by members of a society to bond them together. Societal patterns of marriage—the forms of exchange in which one group of men give women to others—exemplify such gifting, and they are studied by anthropologists to yield underlying structure.[62]

In Freud, "the gift" arises in the need of members of a potential society to bond themselves in a relation of relative equality after they have deposed the tyrranous, pleasure-monopolozing primal father and disposed of his "primal hoard" among themselves. It is the exchange of gifts that prevents the rise of a new tyrant over the young men.

For the structuralists, "the gift" is the Saussurean "signifier"—the material unit associated by convention with a meaning, the token in structural relationships. In a structural reading of Freud such as Lacan's, the manifest contents of unconscious expressions are also signifiers. As such they take on a significance greater than that of merely being the material aspect of the sign: They become units of social exchange. Thus for Lacan as for Vološinov, psychoanalytic phenomena are the products of discourse, the exchange of signifiers. However, where Vološinov stresses discourse's function as the social justification of action, for Lacan, discourse is the means by which a person participates in society and society itself is constituted.

Patient and Therapist

Vološinov recognizes that the psychoanalytic therapy session is a "sui generis social atmosphere," one in which "between doctor and patient there may be differences in sex, in age, in social standing, and, moreover, there is the difference of their professions," not the least of which is the therapist's exclusive possession of the Freudian methodology. It cannot be denied that this is the actual social context in which the "verbal reactions" of psychoanalysis occur, not in an environment somehow abstracted from the social world.

But Vološinov's insistence on the social nature of therapy is accompanied by a view of therapeutic practice that is antithetical to Freud's body of statement—perhaps Vološinov's most serious misreading of Freud:

> The doctor, for his part, aims at enforcing his authority as a doctor, endeavors to wrest confessions from the patient and to compel him to take the "correct" point of view on his illness and its symptoms [p. 78].

[62] See Claude Lévi-Strauss, "Introduction à l'oeuvre de Marcel Mauss," in Marcel Mauss, *Sociologie et Anthropologie* (Paris: Presses Universitaires Francaises, 1966), pp. ix-lii; and Wilden, "Lacan and the Discourse of the Other," pp. 249-284.

Vološinov seems to notice least the stringent precautions with which Freud sought to train future psychoanalytic practitioners to observe and isolate their individual, psychological, and social identities and to control if not annihilate their effects on the therapy. In several papers written in 1912, Freud first demanded that the potential analyst experience a thorough psychoanalysis of his or her own to uncover in his or her own psyche the order of phenomena that he or she would be working with in future patients.

In this same set of papers of "recommendations to physicians practicing psycho-analysis," Freud warned of the phenomenon of "transference" through which the patient attached to the analyst the identities of the persons most involved in the aetiology of his condition.[63] The formation and resolution of such a transference was central to the therapy and required the analyst's understanding in depth. Vološinov feels that the analyst was preoccupied with the meaning of symptoms and their consequences, but as Little Hans's butterfly dream [p. 127] indicates, those symptoms were elucidated only with the patient's own free associations. Whatever the analyst contributed to the explanation of a symptom could only be a paraphrase of the patient's own discovery. It was in the building of the transference, the unarticulated social dynamic between the patient and whoever it was that the analyst came to be for the patient, that the analyst made a singular contribution.

Freud added a theory of the "counter-transference," having learned from his analysis of his own patients that the analyst would place a projection of his own onto the patient that could well interfere with the therapy and its termination,[64] and make the therapist's didactic analysis all the more necessary.

Freud's concern for the transference as a particularly difficult and important manifestation of "unconscious" expression would not, of course, appeal to Vološinov, with his disdain for "the unconscious." But to depict the transference as an extremely subtle, opaque, and inexplicit use of language would suggest its great potential interest—from the perspectives of Freud and Vološinov as well.

Vološinov also criticizes from the point of view of "the unconscious" such crucial terms in the therapeutic relationship as "free association," "resistance," and "censorship," but these do not figure in a confession. So concerned is Vološinov with the unconscious that he confuses "the conscious" with "the explicit," as if everything uttered in the psychoanalytic context must be uttered with a full awareness of meaning and of import for the hearer in order not to be

---

[63] "Recommendations to Physicians Practicing Psycho-Analysis," "On Beginning the Treatment (Further Recommendations on the Technique of Psycho-Analysis, I)," "Remembering, Repeating, and Working-Through (Further Recommendations on the Technique of Psycho-Analysis, II)," and "Observations on Transference-Love (Further Recommendations on the Technique of Psycho-Analysis, III)," trans. James Strachey, in *Standard Edition* 12 (1958): 109-120, 121-145, 146-156.

[64] "Psychogenesis," pp. 144-146.

"unconscious." Free association is not primarily a communication, not a "scenario" for an action, as Vološinov calls discourse. It is itself an act, the labor of the patient's self-discovery. The term "free," as Lacan notes,[65] is ironic, in that the activity is often painful, manual labor.

Because it is labor, it is not surprising that the analyst, contrary to Vološinov's depiction, tends during its progress to remain silent:

> Shall we enquire instead into the source of the subject's frustration? Does it come from the silence of the analyst? A reply to the subject's empty Word, even—or especially—an approving one, often shows by its effects that it is much more frustrating than silence. Is it not rather a matter of frustration inherent in the very discourse of the subject? Does the subject not become engaged in an ever-growing dispossession of that being of his, concerning which—by dint of sincere portraits which leave its idea no less incoherent, of rectifications which do not succeed in freeing its essence, of stays and defenses which do not prevent his status from tottering, of narcissistic embraces which become like a puff of air in animating it—he ends up by recognizing that this being has never been anything more than his construct in the Imaginary and that this construct disappoints all his certitudes? For in this labor which he undertakes to reconstruct this construct *for another*, he finds again the fundamental alienation which made him construct it *like another one*, and which has always destined it to be stripped from him *by another*.[66]

This activity, in which the patient through speech discovers the nature of the images of self and others with which he had peopled his discourse, is no doubt a social activity but, it is so in quite a different sense than that involving Vološinov's confession-wresting and interpretation-forcing analyst. Freud demanded that the analyst know who he or she was for him- or herself, and discover who he or she was for the patient, in order that the patient gain self-knowledge.

Yet undoubtedly this possible sociological meaning of the therapeutic method—and of the theories of language and of civilization—is virtually tacit in the Freudian texts. The fundamental fact of the encounter of Vološinov and Freud remains an irony—that if Vološinov was unable to see how well Freudianism met his demands for a theory of language in society, Freud could see it no better.

After Vološinov and Freud

The Marxist transformation of psychoanalysis that *Freudianism* demands has not occurred; the essence of the psychoanalysis that Freud brought forth has been subjected to every other variety of revision. Evidence for the one is the hesitant, cautious, even self-suspecting tone in which a devoted and painstaking

---

[65] "The Function of Language in Psychoanalysis," p. 10.
[66] *Ibid.*, p. 11.

dialectician, Louis Althusser, introduces "Freud and Lacan" to a Marxist reader-ship.[67] Evidence for the other is the heat of Lacan's invective against revisions of psychoanalysis and the violence of the psychoanalytic reaction against him.

Lacan's first imperative is that the student of psychoanalysis "return to the works of Freud"—to read Freud first and in his entirety, rather than redactions of his work in the writings of his students and commentators.[68] Lacan's own highly condensed and aphoristic style signifies at only one of its levels his refusal to compete with Freud, his desire to stand at a different logical level as a secondary object (or an aftermath) of Freud's works. Except for his clear affirmations of the Freudian texts, he would perhaps fall guilty of the revision he criticizes, even though, to believe him, the cognitive psychology, phenom-enology, and linguistic theory from which he borrows capture the letter of Freud. Likewise, in his epistemological development of three orders of sym-bolization, Lacan intends more for the concept of the sign than he found in Saussure.

The world of psychoanalysis has served as data for modern linguistics, bearing out Vološinov's claim that "Freud's strength lies in having brought these verbal issues pointedly to the fore [p. 24]." The limited quantity of these studies is perhaps the result of Leonard Bloomfield's vigorous injunctions against "men-talism" in linguistic explanations; but major linguists have nonetheless examined the data, and in nonmentalistic ways. Theoretical descriptions of psychological profiles based on structural analysis were written by Edward Sapir and the British linguist J. R. Firth.[69] Charles Hockett, who has anthologized Bloomfield and developed his position for a critique of generative-transformational gram-mar, provided a set of rules for the formation of the material aspect of slips of the tongue that complements Freud's rules for their meanings.[70]

At a point at which the descriptive method of American structural linguistics had matured, Henry Lee Smith, George F. Trager, Norman McQuown, and Hockett worked with the kinesiologist Ray Birdwhistell and several psy-chologists painstakingly to transcribe psychoanalytic interviews. The subtlety of the discourse, embodied in the nuances of its speech and of the meanings signified, provided an extreme test of the delicacy of their transcriptive tools.[71]

[67] "Freud and Lacan," *New Left Review* 55 (1959): 48-65.

[68] "The Function of Language in Psychoanalysis," p. 30.

[69] Edward Sapir, "Speech as a Personality Trait," in *American Journal of Sociology* 32 (1927): 892-905; John R. Firth, "Personality and Language in Society," in *Papers in Linguistics: 1934-51* (London: Oxford University Press, 1957), pp. 176-189.

[70] Charles F. Hockett, "Where the Tongue Slips, There Slip I," in *To Honor Roman Jakobson: Essays on the Occasion of his Seventieth Birthday, 11 October 1966*, Janua Linguarum Series Major 32 (The Hague: Mouton, 1967), 2:910-936.

[71] Robert Pittenger, Charles F. Hockett, and John J. Danehy, *The First Five Minutes: A Sample of Microscopic Interview Analysis* (Ithaca, N. Y.: Paul Martineau, 1960); Norman

The linguist who has most captured the social context of language is William Labov, with painstaking correlations of minute language variation to levels of social class across vast data samples of language users.[72] Given the rigor and thoroughness of Labov's empirical procedures and his insistence on the importance of social text in language study, it is significant that he began the study of discourse analysis with data from therapeutic interviews. Jacqueline Lindenfeld, citing Labov's methodology, has studied the social dynamics of the psychoanalytic cure through changes in syntax by which the patient's and analyst's speech converge in structure.[73] Although Lindenfeld's work is tentative, it seems to be a type of study Vološinov would have endorsed.

The equation of the signifier with the gift and with the role of women, and its application to Freud's sexual theory, has been included in radical critiques of the politics of sexuality in modern Western society, as in the writing of Juliet Mitchell, Julia Kristeva, and Anthony Wilden.[74] For them, political psychology has become a form of semiotics. One of the unexpected results of the equation has been that Freud's theories of sexuality are now viewed less as a kind of moralizing and more as social anthropology.

In two separate areas of inquiry there has been a movement from the individual and the large-scale social focus to a small-scale social focus that has its own particular properties. "Family therapy," seen in the work of Aaron Esterson, puts the very *context* of an individual's psychosis rather than merely the most troubled individual within it—under treatment.[75] The premise of this approach is that an individual cannot be cured unless there is fundamental change in the personal circumstances that brought about his or her disorder—and that the individual typically sent into therapy may not be the person within the family context who most needs the treatment. While Vološinov felt that large-

McQuown, ed., *The Natural History of an Interview*, Microfilm Collection of Manuscripts on Cultural Anthropology, Series 15, Nos. 95-96 (Chicago: Joseph Regenstein Library, University of Chicago, 1971).

[72] *A Quantitative Study of Sound Change in Progress*, United States Regional Survey (Philadelphia, 1972); *Sociolinguistic Patterns* (Philadelphia: University of Pennsylvania Press, 1972); and *Language in the Inner City* (Philadelphia: University of Pennsylvania Press, 1972).

[73] "In Search of Psychological Factors of Linguistic Variation," in *Semiotica* 5 (1972): 350-361.

[74] Juliet Mitchell, *Psychoanalysis and Feminism* (New York: Pantheon, 1974); Julia Kristeva, "Narration and Transformation," *Semiotica* I (1969): 422-448; and Anthony Wilden, "Introduction: The Scientific Discourse: Knowledge as a Commodity," "Critique of Phallocentrism: Daniel Paul Schreber on Women's Liberation," and "The Ideology of Opposition and Identity: Critique of Lacan's Theory of the Mirror-stage in Childhood," in *System and Structure*, pp. 1-30, 278-301, 462-488.

[75] R. D. Laing and Aaron Esterson, *Sanity, Madness and the Family* (London: Tavistock, 1964).

scale historical changes in the position of a class were responsible for the psychopathology of its individual members, the movement away from the strictly individual focus of therapeutic practice lies in his direction.

"Micro-sociology" similarly focuses on small-scale social interaction rather than the large-scale patterns of traditional sociology. Most relevant to Vološinov and Freud is the analysis of underlying rules of procedure in conversation by Harvey Sacks, Emanuel Schegloff, and Gail Jefferson.[76] "Turn-taking," the movement from speaker to hearer among interlocutors, has been revealed to reflect relations of authority between the participants. While this is a study of form rather than ideology, it exposes the complexity and orderliness of social life in discourse.

What these various developments in the interface between the ideas of Vološinov and Freud share is a focus of language and a debt to structural linguistics. That the American structuralists' transcription of therapy sessions is a vastly different use of Saussure than that of the family therapists or of the political analysts of sexual roles (some of whom may have had their initial exposure to Saussure in Lacan's work) only shows that structuralism, the intellectual tendency at the head of which may stand both Freud and Vološinov, is as broad as their shared interest in structure and language is fundamental.

None of these tendencies resolve Vološinov's disagreement with Freud. If Vološinov's condemnation could be replaced by praise, it is only because the intellectual context which gives language, objectivity, and social focus their meaning has changed. And yet the reversal is not to Vološinov's discredit because of a fundamental fact of semiotic life discussed by Lacan:

> I identify myself in Language, but only by losing myself in it like an object. What is realized in my history is not the past definite of what was, since it is no more, or even the present perfect of what has been in what I am, but the future anterior of what I shall have been for what I am in the process of becoming.[77]

Freud might have been as unable to anticipate his structuralist reading as was Vološinov. And the final judgment is not yet in.

---

[76] "A Simplest Systematics for the Organization of Turn-taking in Conversation," in *Language* 50 (1974): 696-734. See also David Sudnow, ed., *Studies on Strategic Interaction* (New York: Free Press, 1972).

[77] "The Function of Language in Psycho-Analysis," p. 63.

Index

and extraverbal situation, 98–101, 105
participants of, 103, 104, 105, 109–116
Verbal reactions, 21, 22–23, 26, 34–35, 80,
85, 87–88
Verbal utterance, 76–78, 86
behavioral/pragmatic, 98–101, 103,
105–106
in literature, 106–108, 110–112, 115
Vološinov, V., vii–xiv, 1–4, 117–125,
129–131, 135–136, 137–140, 142–145,
147–148

W

Watson, J., 18
Weininger, O., 13
Wilden, A., 147
Wish fulfillment, 36, 51
Wittgenstein, L., x, 134
Wundt, W., 18